THE WILD TURKEY TANGO

ANN CHARLES

ILLUSTRATED BY C.S. KUNKLE

"And I thought our Thanksgivings were chaotic. Nothing like a loaded weapon, a turkey, and Thanksgiving cheer all wrapped in a Jeep with three Morgan sisters. The Wild Turkey Tango brings belly laughs to holiday mayhem. Crazy fun!"
~Jacquie Rogers
Author of the Honey Beaulieu – Man Hunter Series

THE WILD TURKEY TANGO

Copyright © 2016 by Ann Charles

All rights reserved. Except as permitted under the U.S. Copyright Act of 1976, no part of this publication may be reproduced, distributed, or transmitted in any form or by any means now known or hereafter invented, or stored in a database or retrieval system, without the prior written permission of the publisher, Ann Charles.

This book is a work of fiction. Names, characters, places, and incidents are the product of the author's imagination or are used fictitiously. Any resemblance to actual persons, living or dead, business establishments, events, or locales is coincidental.

Cover Art by C.S. Kunkle
Cover Design by Sharon Benton
Editing by Mimi the "Grammar Chick"

Printed in the United States of America
First Printing, 2016
Print ISBN: 978-1-940364-42-1

Dear Reader,

As soon as I finished writing *The Rowdy Coyote Rumble*, I knew I had to set aside some time and write the story of the Morgan sisters' Thanksgiving down in Jackrabbit Junction. I could see the turkey feathers flying before I even started Chapter One.

Throughout this novella, I talked often with my good friend and critique partner, Jacquie Rogers. She is an ace at writing funny, action-filled humor, and after years of reading and laughing through her books, I wanted to try my hand at it. Jacquie read as I wrote, cheering me on while snorting and giggling along with me. You can thank her later for the green Jell-O. She told me no Thanksgiving dinner is complete without green Jell-O.

So, without further chatter from me, I'll take my leave and let you enjoy some holiday spirit with Claire, Kate, Ronnie, Chester, and the rest of the Jackrabbit Junction crew. I hope you get some chuckles out of *The Wild Turkey Tango*!

Ann Charles

www.anncharles.com

Also by Ann Charles

Deadwood Mystery Series
Nearly Departed in Deadwood (Book 1)
Optical Delusions in Deadwood (Book 2)
Dead Case in Deadwood (Book 3)
Better Off Dead in Deadwood (Book 4)
An Ex to Grind in Deadwood (Book 5)
Meanwhile, Back in Deadwood (Book 6)
A Wild Fright in Deadwood (Book 7)

Short Stories from the Deadwood Mystery Series
Deadwood Shorts: Seeing Trouble
Deadwood Shorts: Boot Points
Deadwood Shorts: Cold Flame

Jackrabbit Junction Mystery Series
Dance of the Winnebagos (Book 1)
Jackrabbit Junction Jitters (Book 2)
The Great Jackalope Stampede (Book 3)
The Rowdy Coyote Rumble (Book 4)

Goldwash Mystery Series (a future series)
The Old Man's Back in Town (Short Story)

Dig Site Mystery Series
Look What the Wind Blew In (Book 1)
(Starring the brother of Violet Parker—Deadwood Mystery Series)

Coming Next from Ann Charles

Dig Site Mystery Series
Title TBA (Book 2)

Deadwood Shorts
Title TBA (Short Story 4)

Deadwood Mystery Series
Title TBA (Book 8)

*This novella is for my good friend, Jacquie Rogers.
Here is your turkey and green Jell-O.
Enjoy!*

Acknowledgments

As always, the first ones I want to thank for their help and patience are my husband and my kids. The time I spend in front of the computer is taken from the time I would normally spend with them.

Many thanks also to those folks who played a part in making this book go live: my husband, my cover artist, my graphic artist, my editors, my first draft readers, my beta readers, my family and friends, and my brother Clint, on whom I based the turkey's personality. (Ha! Love you, Clint!)

I also want to thank Steppenwolf for their song, *Magic Carpet Ride*. It's the perfect song for tangoing with wild turkeys!

Chapter One

Jackrabbit Junction, Arizona
Thanksgiving Day

"What are you doing with that gun?" Claire Morgan shot a worried glance across the front seat of her Jeep Wrangler at her younger sister, Kate, who was packing heat. "Filling someone's hide full of lead is not on our list of things to do in Yuccaville before tonight's Thanksgiving shindig."

Kate rested the derringer in the palm of her hand. The double barrels were shorter than her middle finger. "It's for protection."

"That's not even real is it?" Claire's older sister asked. Ronnie leaned forward from the backseat, peeking around the headrest. "It looks like a toy."

"It's not a freaking toy." Claire reached across the front seat to push Kate's hands and the tiny pistol away. "Put that damned thing back in your purse before you shoot one of us."

Getting shot was not on her agenda for today. She'd had enough gunplay to last her a lifetime after the last few months in the southeastern Arizona desert.

"It's not even loaded." Kate set the gun on the dashboard. "So relax."

"I'll relax when this Thanksgiving fiasco is over." Claire slowed the Jeep as they reached the Yuccaville city limits. "In the meantime, don't make things worse."

"Oh ye of little faith in me," Kate said, pulling a box of

.22 caliber bullets from her purse and plopping them down on the dash next to the derringer. "Dost thou think I'm totally without brain cells when it comes to a handgun?"

"It's not your intelligence I question," Claire said.

"It's your sanity," Ronnie finished from the backseat. "Where did you get that little gun anyway?"

Claire knew exactly where Kate had found the derringer. "She stole it from Ruby's safe down in the basement office."

The safe actually didn't belong to their stepgrandmother, but rather to her dead husband, Joe Martino—aka Jackrabbit Junction's notorious thief of thieves. The collection of expensive trinkets he'd skimmed over many years of smuggling for nasty sons-a-bitches was stashed all over the house and the Dancing Winnebago R.V. Park. Unfortunately for Claire, she kept stumbling upon

Joe's secret hiding places and finding stolen goods, putting not only her life at risk but her family's lives as well.

"I didn't steal it." Kate pulled a tube of lip balm out of her purse and slathered her lips. "I'm just borrowing it until things calm down and Ronnie can quit walking around squinty-eyed and always watching over her shoulder."

"I'm not squinty-eyed," Ronnie said, squinting out her side window.

Claire followed Ronnie's gaze. A black, late model SUV with dark tinted windows was pulling out of the gas station they were passing. When it turned in the opposite direction, Ronnie settled back into her seat.

Her older sister had good reason to be squinty-eyed. Her ex-husband had played in the sandbox with some big league criminals over the last few years. When the Feds busted him for laundering the big leaguers' money, out came the truth that he'd been embezzling from the felons as well. Now those pissed off goons were hiring hitmen to make Ronnie's ex pay. With her ex-hubby safely tucked away in prison, however, they'd set their sights on what they figured was the next best thing—Ronnie.

Between Joe's tainted legacy and Ronnie's ex, it was only a matter of time before another scorpion crawled out from under a rock and pointed its stinger in the direction of Jackrabbit Junction, aiming to kill.

Claire grimaced at Ronnie in the rearview mirror. "You have been squinting more lately. Maybe you should experiment with your eye makeup, see if there's a way you can make the wrinkles blend in more."

"Good idea." Kate jumped on the bandwagon. "You could line your eyes with dark kohl like Elizabeth Taylor in *Cleopatra*. I'll bet that would make Sheriff Harrison fumble with his handcuffs the next time you two sneak into The Shaft's storeroom to take ol' one eye to the optometrist."

"Ol' one eye to the ..." Claire aimed a furrowed brow

in Kate's direction. "Where'd you hear that one?"

"Chester drove me to the grocery store last night for some mint chocolate chip ice cream. These pregnancy cravings are brutal."

That explained it. Chester was one of their grandfather's bristly old Army buddies whose vernacular barometer rarely rose above "crude with a chance of lewd." He often claimed to be too old to give a damn about what came out of his mouth anymore and was more concerned about the goings-on south of his belt buckle.

"So what if I squint now." Ronnie appeared to be running several conversation beats behind. "Walking around with a target on my back makes sleep a pipe dream most nights."

"Have you tried some sleeping pills?"

"I don't want to take drugs. They might dull my senses and make me even more of a sitting duck."

"You could always take up residence in the Sheriff's bed," Kate suggested.

"Leave Grady out of this." In the rearview mirror, Claire saw Ronnie frown down at her hands. "He has enough stress in his life without adding mine to his plate."

Sheesh, she sure was touchy about the Sheriff lately. That made Claire wonder if something else was going on that Ronnie wasn't sharing with them. The very something the Sheriff had warned Claire about a week ago when he had asked her to keep an eye on Ronnie. It would be typical of her older sister to sit on a potentially explosive secret in order to shield her family from more trouble.

"Maybe the Sheriff would enjoy easing some of your stress." Kate wiggled her eyebrows at Claire and then Ronnie. "If you know what I mean."

Claire snorted. "God, you really need to stop hanging around Chester."

Ronnie's brow creased into a deep V. "It's not Grady's

job to solve my problems for me."

"Fine. Play a hard-ass." Kate held up the derringer, the barrels pointed at the roof. "You could always keep this under your pillow."

"Damn it, Kate." Claire rolled down her window and leaned partway out, putting space between her and her crazy gun-toting sister. "Would you put that dang thing back in your—"

"Look!" Kate pointed the gun at something out her closed window. "Did you see that?"

"Shit-criminy! Don't point that gun out the window!" Claire cursed under her breath. Had she forgotten they were in Arizona? If someone down here saw a gun pointed out the window, they were likely to have a flashback of the O.K. Corral and shoot back.

"What was it?" Ronnie asked, her squint returning as she peered through the glass. "Did you see someone suspicious looking?"

Kate sighed. "No, Ms. Paranoid. I saw a turkey."

A turkey? Claire did a double take at her sister. "This pregnancy is really scrambling your marbles."

"I'm serious. It was a real, flesh and blood turkey. Make a right up there at the next street and circle back. We need to rescue it."

"Kate, look here." Claire grabbed the to-do list Ruby had given her before she'd left the R.V. park and held it toward the space cadet in the passenger seat. "Nowhere on this piece of paper does it say to rescue a live turkey, and there's no time to go chasing tail feathers. We're on a set schedule here thanks to Gramps's stupid mutt."

Earlier this morning, Henry, their grandfather's spoiled beagle, had knocked over the pot in which their mother had been brining the turkey. To make matters worse, Henry then had dragged the bird carcass all over the campground with delusions of grandeur concerning his hunting skills.

Their only hope of having turkey for Thanksgiving now relied on the grocery store in Yuccaville having a fresh one still available.

Kate put the derringer back on the dash and took the list from Claire, pointing at the first item. "It says right there at the top, *fresh turkey*."

"Fresh as in not frozen, Sputnik. Not fresh as in still gobbling." Claire slowed to a stop at the red light. She really hoped the store wasn't out of turkey or they'd have to buy a bottle of Wild Turkey instead and get their mother good and soused so she didn't blow a gasket that her first Thanksgiving in Arizona was a bust.

"I don't care about this silly dinner and don't call me Sputnik." Kate socked Claire in the shoulder. "It's Thanksgiving and I'm going to go rescue that turkey before someone eats it." Before Claire realized what was happening, Kate had climbed out of the Jeep and slammed the door behind her.

"Kate!" Claire yelled at the closed window. "Get back here!"

The light turned green.

Kate waved at her from the sidewalk and headed back in the direction of the turkey.

"She's totally bonkers," Claire said.

A horn honked behind her.

"Bonkers or not, you need to go get her."

"Thank you, back seat driver, but I don't need your help."

The horn honked longer.

"The gas pedal is a pretty basic concept," Ronnie said. "You just push on it and the Jeep will move forward."

"Son of a peach!" Hitting the right blinker, Claire turned down the street Kate had wanted her to take before she'd jumped ship.

Ronnie crawled up into the front seat as they circled the

block. "Over there," she pointed out the windshield. "She headed down the alley behind that smoke shop."

"I could understand chasing down a stray dog, but a turkey? Come on." She frowned at the derringer still sitting on the dash. "Put that damned gun back in Kate's purse before somebody ends up shot."

As Ronnie stuffed the cartridges and gun into the purse, Claire slowed and hit her blinker.

"Not this one, the next." Ronnie grabbed the wheel to keep Claire from turning. She pointed to a gap in the buildings a half a block in front of them.

"I liked it better when you were bossing me around from the back seat." Claire knocked Ronnie's hand off the steering wheel and made a left where her sister still pointed. She noticed the No Outlet sign right before catching sight of Kate's red jacket at the other end of an alley littered with tumbleweeds and plastic bags.

When Claire rolled closer, Kate made a throat cutting motion at her to kill the engine.

Claire shut it down, scowling. "This is a bad idea."

"It's only a turkey."

"Famous last words." She climbed out of the Jeep. "Now what?" she asked Kate, who was slipping off her red jacket.

Kate eyed her Jeep. "Do you have any rope in your toolbox?"

"I have a hammer."

"Don't you dare hurt this poor thing!"

"Kate," Claire tried to reason with her nutty sister, "it's a turkey not a stray cat. You can't take it home, litterbox train it, and snuggle with it on cold nights."

"Have you ever tried training a turkey?" Ronnie joined them.

"Sure," Claire said. "Back when I worked on that wild turkey ranch in Cuckoo-land, we'd catch turkeys all day long and teach them to roll over and play dead."

Ronnie pursed her lips at Claire. "Someone spooned an extra dollop of sarcasm into her coffee this morning."

"Why am I the only one who thinks this is a ridiculous side trip?"

"Because you've lost your Thanksgiving spirit." Kate held her coat out, like she expected to wrap it around the bird and give it a hug.

Claire had plenty of Thanksgiving spirit, starting with the desire to get to the store and find a fresh, non-breathing turkey to roast until it was a beautiful, golden brown delight. Her jeans had loosened over the last week with all of the work she'd been doing cleaning up around the R.V. park. Today, she planned to tighten them back up with plenty of turkey, dressing, and pie. "What do you propose we do if we manage to catch the bird, Kate?"

"Take it out into the boonies and set it free to live the life of the nomad it was meant to be."

"You've been watching too much of the Animal Planet channel."

"Many of the world's animals need our help to survive."

Holy Greenpeace! Impending motherhood along with its heavy doses of hormones had melted Kate's previously cool, somewhat self-absorbed heart into a big beating ball of sensitivity. It often bubbled with so much love these days that it leaked out her eyes in the form of tears.

"I think we should take it to Grady," Ronnie said. "He'll know what to do with it."

"Good idea." For once, Claire didn't wince at the idea of including the law.

"It's a horrible idea!" Kate glared at Ronnie and Claire. "He'll turn it over to the local dog catcher who'll throw it into a little cage—or worse, he'll shoot it and eat it for dinner. Besides, it's illegal to trap and catch wild turkeys out of season."

"Then what the hell are we doing here?" Claire asked.

"We're not trapping or catching it. We're *rescuing* it. Huge difference."

"Kate," Claire squeezed her younger sister's shoulder, trying to be understanding. "I know those baby hormones are taking you on your own version of Mr. Toad's Wild Ride, but try to be reasonable about this. It's just a turkey."

Kate batted away Claire's hand and held her jacket up in front of her, waving the red side toward the turkey. "I am being reasonable. It's dangerous for a turkey to be running around on Thanksgiving. It's our duty as the caretakers of this planet to help all animals without opposable thumbs."

"That's it." Claire threw up her hands. "I officially declare Kate mentally unstable. Ronnie, grab the straitjacket."

Ronnie grabbed Kate's red jacket instead, pulling it out of her hands. "It's not a bull, Katie. There's an easier way to catch a turkey."

There was? "How do you know how to catch a turkey?" Claire asked her older sister.

"This isn't my first turkey roundup." Ronnie flapped Kate's jacket at the bird and ran toward it, yodeling as she attacked.

Claire stood frozen in surprise, watching her usually refined older sister rush the turkey.

The bird let out a series of loud gobbles and shot straight toward the brick wall of the building on their left. It hit the brick head on, and then timbered over like a stately redwood, landing with its feet in the air. Turkey feathers floated around it.

"Ronnie!" Kate stumbled toward the bird, her hand partially covering her mouth. "You killed it!"

Ronnie walked up to the turkey, gently nudging it with her boot. "It's not dead. It knocked itself out cold."

Claire shook free of her surprised stupor and joined her

sisters, peering down at the bird. "Where did you learn that trick? In Cow Tipping 101?"

With a shrug, Ronnie said, "I wasn't the goody two-shoes you've always accused me of being."

Claire grinned. "So in addition to being married to a money launderer, you also wrangled wild turkeys? What other skeletons do you have in that closet?"

After flipping Claire off, Ronnie bent over the turkey and draped Kate's jacket over it.

"Hey! That's my favorite jacket."

"You're the one who wanted to save the wild turkeys of the world." Ronnie wrapped the jacket clear around the bird and then tied the sleeves in a knot to secure the wings. "Let's load this bird up and get rid of it. We need to get back to that list Ruby gave us before all of the freshly dead turkeys at the store are taken. Claire, grab its feet."

"We're not putting the thing in my new Jeep."

"Stop being a fusspot."

"It will poop all over my toolbox and carpet."

"If it does, Katie will clean it up when we get home."

"I already donated my favorite jacket. Can't we tie it to the roof and drive slow until we get out of town?"

Ronnie shook her head at them, her upper lip curled in disgust. "You two are such weenies. Suck it up and let's get this turkey business done."

"Fine, I'll pick up the damned bird," Claire said. Grumbling under her breath, she opened the back of her Jeep and grabbed her brand spanking new expensive leather gloves. "This is insane, you know," she told Kate a minute later as she carried the turkey to the back of her Jeep. "If you weren't pregnant, I'd tie *you* up in your jacket and take you to a mental hospital." She slammed the back of the Jeep closed and pulled off her gloves. "Okay, Mastermind," she said to Ronnie. "Where to now?"

"I caught the danged bird. It's your turn to be the brains

of the operation."

As far as Claire was concerned, catching it had been an example of not using their brains. Now they had a comatose bird in the back and risked getting charged with illegally hunting a turkey and who knew what other fine-incurring offenses if the Sheriff or any of his deputies pulled them over.

She glared at Tweedledee and Tweedledum in turn. "Both of you get in the Jeep before the bird wakes up."

"Katie, you take the back," Ronnie opened the door for her sister.

"Why do I have to ride in back?"

"To be closer to your rescued turkey. Besides, you're pregnant."

"Both of those reasons are total bullshit," Kate said, but climbed into the back seat anyway.

Ronnie handed Kate her purse and slid onto the passenger seat. "So, where are we going?"

"To Dirty Gerties." Starting the Jeep, Claire reversed out of the alley. "Then the grocery store."

"Why are we taking the bird to a strip club?" Ronnie asked as she buckled her seatbelt. "You thinking about having it do the Chicken Dance on stage?"

"A turkey wrangler and a comedian. Your talent appears to be limitless."

"I thought we needed to hurry over to the grocery store before the fresh turkeys are gone," Kate said from the back.

"Dirty Gerties is on the way to the store and stopping there takes care of the second item on our list." Claire hit the gas and headed toward the strip club.

"What's the second item?" they both asked in unison.

"To pick up an even bigger, not-so-fresh turkey."

Chapter Two

Kate needed to use the ladies room. Unfortunately, her two older sisters had left her sitting in the parking lot of a strip club with a bossy order to "watch that turkey" while they disappeared inside to collect a fourth member for their turkey rescue party.

Not that said turkey was doing anything other than sleeping off the concussion Ronnie undoubtedly had caused when she'd chased the poor bird into the brick wall. The last time Kate had checked, the turkey hadn't moved a single feather. Her jacket still held it wrapped up in a sleeved hug.

Opening her purse, she pulled out her cellphone to see if anyone had called or texted. By "anyone" she really meant Butch, who'd been busy working under the hood of a muscle car he'd just acquired from a car auction in El Paso. One would think owning a successful bar and grill like The Shaft, Jackrabbit Junction's main watering hole, would be enough for one man, but not Butch Carter. Oh no, he'd rather get his hands dirty fixing up old cars.

This morning while he was shaving, he'd thrown out the idea of her running The Shaft in his stead. She'd been in the midst of brushing her teeth so her answer had been raised eyebrows of surprise in the bathroom mirror. His ringing phone had saved her from commenting further. If he was serious, she needed some time to think about her answer. While she enjoyed working at The Shaft most days, especially when Butch was there with her, she was uncertain whether she was up to the task of being in charge. She had a definite fear of falling on her face and letting Butch down. She rested her hand on her stomach. Not to mention the changes and adventures their baby would be adding to her world a half year from now.

She shoved the cellphone back into her purse. It clinked against the derringer. She pulled out the little gun, turning it this way and that in the sunlight shining through the back window of the Jeep. Why would Joe Martino have such a little gun? From the way Ruby had described him and his love for greasy food, the man's meaty fingers wouldn't have fit around the trigger whereas Kate's slim finger slid around it just fine.

Her bladder panged again, threatening to overflow. She looked out at Dirty Gerties nondescript white brick building. The doors were still closed, nobody in sight. Leaning back, she tugged at the waistband of her jeans, giving her bladder more room. Those guys needed to hurry their asses up. They'd better not be inside knocking back a few drinks while she sat out here almost peeing her pants with an unconscious turkey for company.

She shifted in the seat and undid her seatbelt, trying to ease the pressure in her midsection even more. Maybe if she stretched out a little. She slid across the seat and turned sideways, resting her right hand with the derringer across the seatback. The handgun was too small to make her look cool holding it. Ronnie was right. It seemed more like a toy.

"Why such a tiny gun, Joe?" she asked aloud.

Holding the derringer up again, she inspected the mother-of-pearl inlay on the handle. With the sun shining on it, she could see carved designs that she hadn't noticed before when looking at it down in the shadow-filled basement office.

A choked gobble came from behind her seat.

Kate squawked, too, almost peeing her pants. She

leaned over the back of the seat slowly, her hands shielding her in case the turkey had somehow freed itself and decided to attack.

It lay unmoving on the floor where Claire had put it in the back of the Jeep. The jacket's sleeves were still wrapped around it.

What in the heck had she heard? The bird's ghost? Had it passed over into the turkey afterlife?

She reached down with the derringer. Holding her breath, she poked the bird's breast with the gun barrels.

Nothing moved.

Hmm. Maybe she'd imagined ...

The turkey sprang to life in a loud gobble-squawk, its head twisting this way and that. Before Kate could snap out of her frozen state of surprise, it strained upward and pecked her wrist.

"Yowch!" When Kate yanked her hand back, her finger hit the trigger of the derringer.

A gunshot exploded inside the vehicle.

Five minutes later ...

"You have got to be freaking kidding me!" Claire stood behind her Jeep. She frowned at the bullet hole now gracing the thick black vinyl next to the back window of the soft top. "You shot my new Jeep!"

"It was an accident," her younger sister insisted. Kate reached out and poked her pinkie finger into the hole.

"Don't do that. You're going to make the hole even bigger." Claire pulled Kate's hand back and then leaned closer to inspect the damage. "Shit. Mac is probably going to get those deep vertical lines in his forehead when he sees this."

"It's a tiny hole. He won't even notice it."

"He will too." Her boyfriend didn't miss much, especially when it came to anything related to Claire and her sisters.

"I'll see if Butch can get it patched up."

"Do you really want the father of your unborn child to know you were playing with a loaded gun?"

"I wasn't playing with it. I told you it was an accident." When Claire continued to stare her sister down, she added, "It's the turkey's fault."

"Oh, it's a turkey's fault all right, the turkey that goes by the name of Crazy Kate." Claire pointed at the gun that now lay next to the turkey in the back of her Jeep. "I thought you said that damned gun wasn't loaded."

"I didn't think it was." Kate kept shifting from one foot to the other. "I certainly didn't put any bullets in it."

Chester Thomas joined them, his gray hair and matching beard stubble looking extra bristly. Must be one of the dancers at Dirty Gerties had gotten him all excited, or maybe it was the owner, to whom he seemed to give a lot of extra attention these days. "Ronnie says you need my help out here with some sexy bird you picked up with a meaty set of breasts and cute tail feathers."

In spite of the bullet hole in her ride, Claire grinned at her sister's trickery. That was a sure-fire way of getting Chester's attention. "Where is Ronnie?"

"She needed to use the latrine."

"So do I," Kate said. "I'll be right back."

As soon as Kate left, Chester turned to Claire. "Where's this sexy bird?"

Claire looked pointedly toward the back of the Jeep.

It took Chester a full three seconds of ogling to soak up the truth of the matter. "What in the hell are you girls doing with a wild turkey?"

"Kate decided to rescue it."

"It's not dead?" When Claire shook her head, he asked, "Where did you find it?"

"It was running around town. Kate tracked it down, Ronnie wrangled it, and now I'm stuck hauling it."

He rubbed his hand over his stubbly jaw. "What are you going to do with it?"

"Kate wants to take it out in the desert and set it free."

"That might be a death sentence. Water isn't exactly sitting around in puddles out here. Why does it look dead?"

"Kate just shot at it by accident with the derringer." She pointed to where the small gun now lay next to the turkey, where Claire had insisted Kate leave the weapon so she didn't shoot anything else. "She thinks it passed out from fear when it heard the gun blast."

"I thought I heard a gunshot over the dance music, but I figured it was just a pickup backfiring." He palmed the derringer. "Where'd she get the pea shooter?"

"Joe's safe. Kate insists she didn't load the gun, so he must have kept one in the chamber." When Claire thought of the times she'd gotten into that safe and moved the gun around, it made her stomach clench. All of this time it had been loaded. Jeez, they were lucky nobody had gotten shot, including the damned turkey.

Chester opened the chamber and dumped the casing out onto the ground, then peered down the barrels. "It's empty now." He picked up the tattered box of cartridges Kate had taken out of her purse and set it next to the derringer. "Pregnant women bursting with hormones should not be allowed to touch firearms." He opened the box and dumped a few of the cartridges out on the carpet next to the turkey. "Arizona should make that into a law."

Normally, her feminist side bucked at such talk, but in Kate's case, Claire agreed one hundred percent. "What are you doing?"

"Just checking out this little palm pistol." He grabbed a

cartridge and stuck the bullet into one of the two barrels. "Step back, I'm going to see how true she shoots."

"You're what?" Claire reached for the gun. "You can't shoot it here. That's illegal."

"Who's gonna tell? Around here, folks don't think twice about loud bangs what with the mine blowing up the hillsides every other night." He took a couple of steps toward the wide open dirt lot next to them and aimed at the ground.

Claire plugged her ears and pinched her eyelids closed. She waited for the bang of the gun, which would undoubtedly be followed by the Sheriff department's sirens.

She stood like that for about five seconds but nothing happened. She unplugged her ears and opened her eyes. Chester had the derringer open again and was frowning down at the small barrels.

"What's wrong?" she asked, keeping her distance.

"It didn't fire." He walked back to her. "Hold this." He handed her the unspent cartridge and grabbed a few more from the box.

Loading another round in the chamber, he aimed and pulled the trigger.

Nothing happened.

He emptied the gun, reloaded, and tried twice more. Both times ended with a click, nothing more.

"Hell, none of these rounds are lighting up." He took several more and went through the same routine. By the time he finished, with still no shots fired, Ronnie and Kate had returned.

"What's going on?" Kate asked.

Ronnie's gaze moved from the collection of cartridges in Claire's hand to where Chester was unloading another one. "Is he actually trying to shoot the gun?"

"Yep."

"Damned rounds are all duds." Chester returned and set

the gun down, pointing it away from them. "Where did you get this box of rounds, Katie?"

"Next to the derringer in the safe."

"They were there the first time I opened the safe," Claire added.

He held one of the cartridges up in the light, squinting at it. "Doesn't make any sense that they'd all be duds."

"They weren't." Kate pointed at the bullet hole she'd made in the Jeep's soft top. "Do bullets have expiration dates?"

"Joe's only been dead a couple of years," Claire reminded her.

"Maybe he had them for a lot longer."

"Or maybe they're as old as the gun." Ronnie leaned closer to the bullet hole, aiming her finger at it.

Claire grabbed her by the wrist. "Keep your fingers to yourself."

"You sound like Mom," Kate said.

"It's just a tiny hole. Katie told me inside that she didn't mean to do it."

"How much did she pay you to take her side?" Claire asked Ronnie.

"She promised a five-er."

"Wow, you're cheap."

"There's something wrong with these rounds," Chester said.

"They're duds, I know. I was standing here while you were trying to shoot up the place, remember?"

"I mean something else." He walked over to Claire and held up a cartridge for her to inspect.

"It looks like a bullet to me."

"Check out the base of the tip."

She scratched her chin. "I'm relatively new to bullets, Chester. What am I looking for here?"

"The gap between the case and the bullet."

"What about it?"

"This one is loose, see?" He pulled, widening the gap between them. "I'd pull harder, but my damned arthritis makes it hard to pinch."

"You don't seem to have trouble with pinching when it comes to the girls at Dirty Gerties."

"That's called willpower," he said with a wink.

Claire took the cartridge from him and pulled. The bullet popped right off in her fingers.

She'd expected gun powder to spill out. Instead, a little piece of rolled up paper fell onto the ground.

Ronnie reached down and grabbed it before the wind got hold of it and carried it away to the weed-filled lot. She unrolled the tiny piece of paper.

"Does it say anything?" Claire asked, moving close to take a look.

"Yes."

"What?" Kate joined them.

Ronnie frowned up at Chester and then Kate, her focus landing on Claire last. "It says, *X marks the spot.*"

"It sounds like some kind of pirate game," Kate said, excitement making her voice breathy.

"Ah, hell," Claire muttered, rubbing her hand over her eyes. "Here we go again."

Chapter Three

Claire opened several more cartridges, handing each piece of paper with the exact same words to Kate to hold.

"They're like fortune cookie bullets," Kate said.

Ronnie cocked her head to the side. "Why do they all say the same thing?"

"Who cares?" Kate cupped her hands when a breeze tried to blow the papers free. "What treasure do you think is underneath the X?"

Claire smirked. She'd been there and done that with Joe and his hide-and-seek games enough times to know it couldn't be as simple as finding a spot on a map. "There is no treasure under the X."

Ronnie stuffed the bullets and casings she'd collected back into the cartridge box. "You sound pretty certain about that."

"I'm ninety-nine percent sure."

"Why?"

"Because X never marks the spot," Chester horned in between Kate and Ronnie. "Haven't you learned anything from Indiana Jones?"

"I wasn't the TV addict. That was Claire."

"Indiana Jones is from a movie, numbskull," Claire told Ronnie. "Not TV."

"A movie that they now play on TV stations, right, buttinski?"

"Enough, you two," Kate stepped between them.

Ronnie traded Chester the box of empty cartridges for the derringer. "You can keep track of these, Katie can keep the fortunes, and I'll keep the derringer in the front seat away from you and our deranged turkey lover." She stuffed the tiny gun into her back pocket.

Chester slipped the box into the side pocket of his cargo pants. "That's a bad place to keep a gun."

"So is Katie's hands," she replied. "And yours."

Kate stuffed the tiny papers into her purse. "Claire, how can you be so sure there's no treasure?"

"Because Joe's treasure hunts are never as simple as an X on a map." Nope, Joe was a master pirate. And here all of this time she'd figured that box of cartridges went with the derringer. Now she was beginning to suspect they might be related to two different skims he'd made during his time as a thief of thieves.

Ronnie crossed her arms over her chest. "So what do we do now?"

"We go to the store and pick up a dead turkey and then grab what's next on our list," Claire pulled the Jeep keys from her back pocket. Whatever game Joe had been playing with that box of cartridges could wait until after they had made it through this damned day. She hoped with all of the hormones swirling around in Kate's head she'd soon forget about the weird messages and move on with life. Otherwise, they would be screwed because Kate was part badger these days. When she sank her teeth in, she refused to let go. Period.

"Don't you want to figure out why he filled bullets with little papers instead of gun powder?" Kate pointed at Chester's pants. "*That* means something and you know it."

Chester chuckled. "Are we talking about the rounds in my pocket or the other treasures in my britches?"

After rolling her eyes and shaking her head at Chester, Claire told Kate, "Maybe. Maybe not. But today isn't the day to go digging around the R.V. park. Shooting a hole in my Jeep is enough of an adventure for one day, Calamity Jane." She shut the tailgate and walked around to the driver's door. "Now let's go get *another* turkey."

Fifteen minutes later ...

Unfortunately, when Mother Hubbard went to the grocery store cupboard, the only turkeys there were still frozen solid. When Chester joined Claire at the cash register, he had a twelve pack of cheap beer under one arm and a big can of *chili con carne* under the other.

"Where's the turkey?" he asked.

"I'm looking at him." She pointed at his groceries. "You running low on breakfast supplies?"

"These are my contributions to Thanksgiving potluck—drinks and a side dish."

"Butch is going to have beer on tap, remember?" This year's dinner was being held on the back patio at The Shaft, where the beer and liquor were plentiful.

"That shit's too yuppie for my taste."

"You didn't seem to mind it the other night."

"Your grandfather was buying. When the cheap bastard forks out cash, I put aside my finer tastes. Where's the turkey you were supposed to be grabbing?"

"They're sold out of fresh ones. Butch offered to serve us burgers, same as the locals coming who haven't anywhere else to go. Right now, that sounds good enough for me."

Chester grinned. "Burgers go great with *chili con carne* piled on 'em."

They paid and headed out, filling Ronnie and Kate in on the store's turkey situation.

"Mother is going to blow a gasket," Ronnie said.

"It wouldn't be Thanksgiving if she didn't bitch and moan about something." Claire looked across the front seat at Ronnie. "What's next on the list?"

Ronnie plucked the piece of paper from the cup holder. "Pick up the pies."

"Butch said there should be five of them boxed and ready at the Mule Train Diner," Kate told them.

"I didn't realize Grady's sister made pies for the public," Ronnie said.

"She doesn't usually. She donates them to The Shaft's free Thanksgiving dinner Butch puts on each year."

"That's nice of her," Ronnie said, frowning out the window yet again.

Claire glanced over at her older sister before rolling out of the parking lot. "Something wrong with that?"

Ronnie shrugged. "When it comes to Grady's family, I feel like a black sheep."

"How's that different than where you fit in with your own family?" Chester asked from the backseat.

"Katie," Ronnie said without turning around, "pinch Chester for me, please."

In the rearview mirror, Claire saw Kate elbow the old goat instead.

Claire slowed and made a left turn. The diner was a few blocks ahead.

"It's just that Grady's family seems perfect, like characters from *The Andy Griffith Show*," Ronnie said. "I don't fit in there amongst the Mayberry folks."

Chester guffawed. "You'd blend in better on *Hee Haw* if you ask me. Especially with Daisy Mae here being knocked up by the local moonshine runner and all of the inbreeded marrying going on in your family these days."

"Can it, peanut gallery." Kate yanked on his ear hard enough to make him yelp.

Claire pulled into a parking spot in front of the diner and then turned to her older sister. "You seem to be forgetting about the Sheriff's niece trading cheap sex for self-confidence."

"And don't forget his Aunt Millie," Kate said, leaning forward.

"Ronnie, I know you like Grady's aunt," Claire said, "but keep in mind that Millie is a racketeering queen and extortionist extraordinaire, organizing all sorts of small crimes from the library to the senior center."

"Not to mention a bully."

Ronnie frowned at Kate. "She didn't even touch you, ya big baby."

"Anyway," Claire continued, "don't let Grady's shiny badge fool you. His family is as tarnished and screwed up as everyone else's; he just has the power in this town to point his finger and make his accusations stick."

"And throw innocent victims in jail," Kate added.

"Spare us the melodrama, Scarlett O'Hara," Claire told Kate. "You locked yourself in that cell the last time."

"Are one of you three going to go get those pies sometime before I wither up and die back here?"

"Hold your horses, Chester," Claire said.

"It's not my horses I'm worried about, it's my prostate."

"I haven't met Grady's sister officially yet," Ronnie said, flipping down the visor and checking her face in the mirror. "Do I look okay?"

Claire smirked. "You're having sex with her brother, Ronnie, not looking for her permission to marry him." She pushed open her door. "Chester, keep an eye on Calamity Kate and her new pet. I don't need any more so-called accidents in my Jeep."

Kate blew a raspberry at Claire. "It's one teeny tiny hole."

"Let's keep it that way."

Lucky for Ronnie, Grady's sister wasn't in the diner. She'd gone home to start their family's festivities.

"Great," Ronnie whispered as the woman behind the counter went in back to collect the pies from the walk-in cooler. "His family probably hates me for taking him away from them this holiday."

"You're just looking for a reason to beat yourself up today, aren't you?"

"I guess so."

"Well, knock it off. You said Grady always worked the holiday, so as far as they're concerned, nothing is out of the ordinary."

"Except that his Aunt Millie will be gracing our table instead of theirs."

"I have a feeling that's a blessing for them. They should be thanking you."

The woman came back with five pie boxes. Claire's stomach rumbled at the cherry pie glistening through the cellophane window as she carried three stacked pies toward the door. Ronnie balanced the other two and led the way outside.

"Why don't you put them in back?" Chester asked when Ronnie opened his door and handed him two to hold on his lap.

"Have you forgotten about Count Turk-ula conked out back there?"

"Oh, yeah. When are we going to ditch that bird, anyway?"

"As soon as we get outside of town," Kate answered, taking two of the pie boxes Claire handed her through the back seat window.

"Have you considered that you're taking it away from its family on Thanksgiving, Katie?" Ronnie winked at Claire, and then she buckled her seatbelt and settled the last pie on her lap.

"I'm not a six-year-old bee killer anymore, Ronnie," Kate said, referring to the time Ronnie had convinced her that killing a bee would make its family starve and had made Kate give it a proper bee funeral. "The only thing I'm taking it away from is the dog-catcher's dinner table."

Claire started the Jeep and headed toward Main Street. "What's next on Ruby's list?" she asked Ronnie.

"The last thing says, *Stay out of jail.*"

Kate scoffed. "Ha ha. Real funny, Ronnie."

"I'm serious." Ronnie leaned forward and cranked up the stereo as Steppenwolf's *Magic Carpet Ride* started with its telltale whiny electric guitars. "I love this song," she hollered above the music.

Claire turned down the volume a little as Steppenwolf really got to jamming. "It really says that on the list?"

"Yep." Ronnie held up the paper.

Claire glanced over as she paused at the Stop sign before making a right onto Yuccaville's main drag. The handwriting on the last item was different from Ruby's, who'd written the rest of the list. "That last one looks like Gramps's writing."

She hit the gas and headed toward Jackrabbit Junction.

"You sure it's not Mac's?" Kate said and let out a cackle-snort laugh. "How many times has he bailed you out of jail now?"

Said the kettle, Claire thought, frowning at her fellow inmate in the rearview mirror. The sight of a second head sticking up behind Kate's made her do a double take.

"Turkey!" She shouted it more in surprise than warning.

"You're the turkey," Kate shot back.

As if understanding that it was the butt of the insult, the turkey looked over at Kate. Its reddish-pink snood and wattle jiggled as it stared her up and down.

"Claire, watch out!" Ronnie shouted.

Claire looked out the windshield, veering to the left to

avoid sideswiping a dually pickup with its tail end sticking out into the street.

When she glanced back in the rearview mirror, the turkey's head was gone. Had she imagined that? Was she having pre-Thanksgiving dinner hunger hallucinations?

She checked the road in front of her and then looked into the mirror again as Kate opened the lid of one of the pie boxes, licking her lips. "These pies smell as delicious as they look."

"Don't open that," Claire said. "You'll get hair in it."

A turkey head popped up next to Kate's right ear. Before Claire could get a word out, the bird leaned over and locked its beak onto her sister's earlobe.

An eardrum-piercing scream rang out.

Then all hell broke loose.

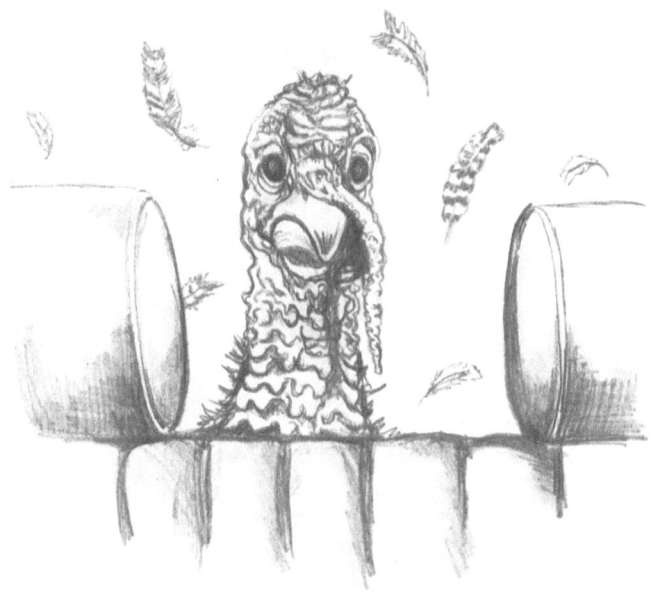

Chapter Four

"Somebody grab that damned turkey!" Claire yelled amidst the cacophony of screeches and shouts and gobbles and squawks.

Feathers flew everywhere.

Wincing and ducking, dodging a face-full of tail feathers, Claire tried to steer the Jeep along Yuccaville's main drag without running into a light pole, another car, or worse.

The turkey's head popped between the front seats. Ronnie let out a shriek and tried to smack it with the pie she'd been holding in her lap. The apple pie slid right out of the box and landed upside down in a heap in Claire's lap.

"Ronnie!"

The turkey evaded the pie box when Ronnie swung it around again, and then tried to take a piece out of Claire's shoulder in retaliation. Claire yelped in pain and surprise, pressing her body against the door to escape its snapping beak. Chester grabbed the bird by the neck and yanked it into the back seat again.

A loud gobbled screech made Claire grimace. A yip of pain from Chester followed. "That goddamned birdie bit me in my family giblets!"

"For crissake, Ronnie," Claire shouted over the chorus of *Magic Carpet Ride*. "Get back there and help them!"

Ronnie unbuckled her seatbelt and turned around in her seat to help. "Katie, catch it by the neck!"

Another shriek rang out from Kate.

"Get that pie! No, grab its wing! Quit worrying about what's in your hair!" Ronnie barked orders from the helm.

"It's got my finger!" Kate cried. "Owie, owie, owie!"

Claire looked in the mirror and saw nothing but feathers as Kate tried to shake free from the turkey's hold.

Chocolate pie filling flew past Claire's headrest and splatted on the steering wheel.

What the hell? Claire growled. Not the chocolate pie, too, dang it.

A turkey wing flapped next to her head, smacking her in the ear several times. She put up her hand, blocking and smacking it back.

"Red light!" Ronnie yelled, pointing out the windshield.

Too late.

Claire sailed through the red light while trying to dodge and peer around the turkey wing that kept flapping in her face and blocking her vision.

"Somebody get this damned bird out of my way!" Claire bellowed. Ronnie caught the bird by the tail and tossed it into the back seat again just as an ancient, tank-like van backed out into the street in front of them. Claire swerved toward the center line, nearly shaved the van's bumper, then almost careened straight into the grill of a white Bronco. She jerked the wheel, sending Ronnie hurtling into her.

Claire's head smacked into the side window hard enough to jar her teeth. "Jeeeezus, Ronnie!"

"That was your fault." Her sister pushed back upright in her seat.

"Hold the blasted wheel steady, girl!" Chester hollered from the debacle in the back of the Jeep. "You just dumped the cherry pie in my lap."

"Excuse me," she shouted back, "while I try not to kill us all!" As soon as they made it outside of the city limits she was pulling over and getting that damned turkey out of her Jeep.

Ronnie leaned between the seats into the back, her butt now bumping into Claire's shoulder. "I got its leg," she said. "Chester, get the other one."

Out of nowhere, a black pickup pulled out from Claire's left, aiming right for her door. She punched the gas to avoid being T-boned.

With a cry of alarm, Ronnie fell into the backseat, her legs now the only thing up front with Claire.

"It's biting my butt!" Ronnie said between yaps of pain. "Katie, grab the stupid bird!"

"I can't! You're pinning down my arms."

"I'm going to snap its scrawny neck for messing up a perfectly good cherry pie," Chester hollered above the noise of Steppenwolf's guitar riffs.

"Don't kill it!" Kate cried. "It's just scared."

A wild flurry of flapping followed. More pie was flung into the front—landing on the dash and the windshield. Even the rearview mirror took a hit. Screeches, squawks, and more cries of pain made Claire's ears ring. Three more blocks and this magic carpet ride was over!

"I got it!" Ronnie yelled.

"Hold that feisty pecker still," Chester said.

Claire looked in the rearview mirror in time to see Chester hit the turkey over the top of the head with an empty pie pan.

Silence filled the Jeep.

"You killed it," Kate whispered.

"Nah, I just knocked it out."

"Would somebody help me get my face out of this damned pecan pie!" Ronnie's voice was muffled.

Claire breathed a sigh of relief as they reached open desert and rolled down the window to let some of the feathers out.

The sound of a siren blared through the open window. "Shit!"

Claire pulled off the road. "Nobody says a word, got it?" She glared at Kate and Chester in the rearview mirror. It was more of a command than a question. "I'll handle this."

"Please tell me that's not Grady," Ronnie said from her pecan pie plate, trying to wiggle her butt back into the front seat. Her sneaker hit the radio volume button. *Magic Carpet Ride* rock-and-rolled from the speakers.

A glance in the side mirror confirmed her sister's nightmare. Sheriff Grady Harrison was walking their way. The song ended right as the Sheriff filled her window. She turned off the radio and waited for the next shit storm to hit.

Grady rested his forearms on the sill and peered inside, his focus shifting from Claire to Ronnie's butt, which was sticking up between the seats with the damned derringer poking halfway out of her pocket. A deep, rippling V formed on his forehead. His gaze moved, first to Chester's side of the backseat and then Kate's. As he took in the scene, the lines around his mouth doubled.

"Afternoon, Sheriff," Chester broke the silence. "Your sister makes a deeee-licious cherry pie." Claire glanced over her shoulder and watched him dig his finger in the mashed up mess of cherry goodness he'd scooped back into the pie plate and then pop the dab of pie filling into his mouth.

Hells bells! Claire had wanted a piece of that pie.

Ronnie grabbed the side of Claire's seat and struggled back into the front. Twisting around, she forced an extra-wide smile through a face covered with pecan pieces, pie goop, and bits of crust. "Hi, Grady!"

"Tone it down about a hundred watts there, sunshine," Claire muttered.

The Sheriff lowered his sunglasses, his narrowed gaze bouncing between Ronnie and Claire. A feather floated in front of his face and out the window. When he finally spoke, his gravelly voice was edged with exasperation. "I don't even know where to start on this one."

Claire did ... maybe. "There's a perfectly good explanation for this."

His lips twitched at the corners. "This should be good."

Ronnie brushed pecan pie crust off her face while she waited along with Grady to hear Claire's "perfectly good explanation." She was glad her sister was taking control of the situation, because short of lifting her shirt to distract Grady while the rest made a run for it, Ronnie couldn't think of another way to get them out of trouble at the moment.

"Uhhhh," Claire started, staring up at Grady's stony expression. His badge glinted in the sunlight.

Ronnie held her breath, willing her sister not to let Grady's stare-down routine ruffle her feathers. If anyone could handle the Sheriff, it was Claire.

Her sister pointed in Ronnie's direction. "The turkey rustler can explain it all."

What a lowdown, stinking brat! Ronnie gaped at Claire and then pinched her sister's thigh for good measure. "Backstabber."

Grady's focus shifted to Ronnie. "Turkey rustler?"

She'd planned to impress Grady later today with her hostess abilities and refined etiquette at the dinner table, hoping to show him she wasn't really the unruly, immoral lawbreaker type she'd appeared to be over the last month. But now here she sat with egg on her face. A piece of crust fell off of her cheek onto her shirt. Make that pie on her face.

"Well ..." She licked her lips and tasted brown sugar.

After wrestling a freaked out turkey, she was too distracted to come up with any justification for the chaos that had just ensued.

One of Grady's eyebrows inched up as he waited.

She squared her shoulders. She could fit into his Mayberry lifestyle, dammit. She just needed a chance to prove it—along with a shower and some new clothes. But first ... she pointed her thumb back at her youngest sister. "It all started when Katie kidnapped a wild turkey."

"What!!?" came from the backseat, followed by, "You two are nothing but big mouthed tattletales!"

A slice of chocolate pie flew from the backseat and splattered onto Ronnie's cheek.

She gasped. Scooping up the chocolate mess from where it had slid onto her shoulder, she threw it back at Katie.

"Stop throwing pie in my Jeep!" Claire yelled at the two of them.

Katie wiped the chocolate pie goop from her chin. "I can't believe how easy you just rolled over on me, Ronnie. Whatever happened to family comes first?"

Family did still rule for Ronnie, but she figured Grady was less likely to throw a pregnant woman in jail than her or Claire. "Calm down and stop acting so crazy," she said quietly, trying to diffuse Katie before the wild monkeys in her sister's head started shrieking and flinging poo as well as pie. "Especially in front of the Sheriff."

"I'll show you crazy," Katie said, scooping up another handful of chocolate pie.

"Kate, don't!" Claire said, glaring her down in the rearview mirror. "If you throw that, I'm going to come back there and give you a chocolate pie noogie."

"This is starting to remind me of the mud pit at Dirty Gerties," Chester chuckled. "I'll wager a ten spot on Ronnie. I've seen her take down a young strapping buck and hogtie him in the blink of an eye like a rodeo superstar."

With a "harrumph," Katie reached over and smeared the handful of chocolate pie down Chester's cheek. "Wager on that, old man!"

"That's it!" Grady's voice resonated through the cab. He yanked open Claire's door. "Everyone out, now!"

Claire and Ronnie exchanged worried glances and then stepped out into the sunlight. Katie and Chester joined their huddle behind the Jeep after dumping the turkey into the back again. They lined up along the shoulder while Grady took his favorite wide-legged Sheriff stance and glared them down one by one.

A semi-truck rolled past, laying on his horn while he waved at them. A tail wind blew along behind him, coating their sticky pie stains with road dust. Ronnie scrubbed her face with the hem of her T-shirt, grimacing at the dirt and pie that came off. That stupid turkey had really done a number on them.

She glanced at Katie, who was going to need to be pre-soaked before going through a hose-down. The poor girl had been at ground zero when the turkey had gone wild on them. Her blonde hair was smeared with chocolate and cherry pie filling. Her face and neck were splotchy with the goop, too. Mixed in with the smudges of pie and crust were scratches from the turkey's claws. Dried blood crusted the bottom of her earlobe.

Chester had fared better. While his clothes were a mess, he seemed relatively unscathed besides the chocolate swipe Katie had left on his cheek and the cherry filling caught in his beard scruff. He offered Ronnie a bite from the pan with the remains of the cherry pie in it. When she shook her head, he shrugged, picking out a feather and tossing it aside while scooping up another piece for himself.

The least damaged from the killer turkey attack was

Claire with only a few pie splotches and one scratch down the side of her face. Unfortunately, her new Jeep showed the results of the multiple pie fatalities.

Grady held up his finger. "I'll be right back. Nobody move."

While Grady strode to his Bronco, Claire stepped over to peek in through Chester's window at the back seat.

"The Sheriff said not to move," Chester said and then popped a cherry in his mouth.

Claire stalked back and stole the pie from him. "I'm going to kill that freaking turkey," she growled in Katie's direction as she dug out a finger full of pie. "That bird better not have torn my seats, you bleeding-heart bozo."

Katie lifted her chin. "This was not the turkey's fault."

Claire scoffed, shoving the cherry pie back at Chester. "You should have shot it when you were waving that damned gun around."

Grady must have heard her, because as soon as he returned he nailed Ronnie with a squint. "Veronica, give me that derringer sticking out of your back pocket."

She handed it over. It looked silly in his large palm.

He flipped it one way and the other, and then nailed her with a frown. "Where did you get this?"

"Katie got it out of Ruby's safe," she told him.

Katie punched her in the arm. "Would you quit blaming me for everything, you rat."

"It belonged to Joe," Claire clarified.

"Maybe you should arrest Miss Big Mouth here for carrying a firearm," Katie suggested, still glaring at Ronnie.

"We're in Arizona, sweetheart," Chester said, licking cherry goop off one of his fingers. "The land of guns and sunshine. It's not illegal for Ronnie to have a firearm on her person."

"That's true." Grady's attention remained on Ronnie. "But riding around with one stuffed in your back pocket is a surefire way to get shot in the ass."

"It's not loaded," Ronnie told him.

He double-checked her claim. "I see that." He closed his fingers around the little handgun. "So which one of you clowns put the bullet hole in the back of Claire's Jeep?"

Ronnie shared a worried glance with Katie before facing off with Grady again. "You don't miss a thing, do you, Sheriff?"

He lowered his sunglasses, eyeballing her over the top of the lenses. "Not when it comes to you, Veronica Morgan."

A blast of heat washed over her that had nothing to do with the bright rays of Arizona sunshine warming her shoulders.

"Let's make a deal, Sheriff," Chester said, ruining the moment. "You take Ronnie in exchange for our freedom."

Katie snorted. "That's no deal when she goes to him willingly already."

"I don't know," Grady said, pushing his sunglasses back up and studying each of them in turn, starting with Claire. "The list of crimes is long this afternoon, with running a red light, crossing over the center line, reckless driving, and speeding for starters."

He moved to Ronnie. "Then there's not wearing a seatbelt and reckless endangerment with a firearm."

His attention shifted to Katie. "Not to mention hunting wild turkey out of season."

Chester snorted. "It sounds to me like you should take all three of these hoodlums to jail while I skip along on my merry way."

Katie jammed her hands on her hips. "Really, Chester? And what about when you attempted to discharge a firearm at Dirty Gerties?"

Grady pushed his hat back and scrubbed at his forehead before yanking the brim down again. "What do you mean attempted?"

"The bullets were all duds," Ronnie explained.

Claire elbowed her, shaking her head at Ronnie.

"How many rounds did you attempt to fire?" he asked Chester.

"I lost count."

"Seven," Katie supplied. When Chester squinted at her, she said, "What? If we go to jail, you're going with us this time, buster."

"How is it all seven rounds were duds?"

Each of them looked elsewhere, avoiding Grady's scrutiny. If this went any further, they'd have to give up their secret about a possible buried treasure.

"Chester?" Grady pressed.

The old buzzard wiped the cherry goop off his face with his shirt sleeve. "I'd like to request the presence of my attorney before I answer that."

A loud gobble-squawk came from the back of the Jeep. They all turned as the turkey poked its head out of Chester's open window.

After a raucous fluttering of feathers and wings, the turkey hopped up on the window sill. With a dismissive squawk in their direction, it made a leap to freedom, landing in the ditch next to a collection of tumbleweeds that waited for the next strong breeze. Then it was off, racing like the Roadrunner across the open desert valley toward the western horizon.

"Free bird!" Katie yelled after it, holding both hands in the air with a two-fingered peace gesture. Ronnie shook her head. The remaining members of Lynyrd Skynyrd would have been so proud.

"Okay you Keystone Kops." Grady's voice rippled with an undercurrent of laughter. "We've reached the end of today's episode of *The Wild Turkey Tango*. Now, which one of you is going to spill your big secret?"

Ronnie hesitated, weighing how big of a deal it would be if Grady knew about Joe's *X marks the spot* message. She didn't want him put in the position again of dealing with the aftereffects of Joe's criminal acts, especially with everything else he was balancing thanks to the hitmen her ex-husband's goons kept siccing on her.

"Well, then." The Sheriff crossed his arms over his chest. "If nobody feels like talking, I guess all four of you win a free trip with me back to the station until we can sort out this whole mess."

Chapter Five

Two seconds later ...

"The bullets were filled with clues," Kate blurted.

"Kate!" Claire nailed her sister with the stink-eye.

"What? I don't want to go to jail. It always gives me a rash. Plus, I promised Butch I'd open the bar today and by the time I help clean up your Jeep, I'll be running late."

"I told you the last time we were in Sheriff Harrison's holding tank that those were just hives." Claire blew out a sigh of frustration. Now the law was going to be paying a visit to the Dancing Winnebago R.V. Park, sniffing around and digging up truths she'd rather keep hidden for Ruby's sake.

The Sheriff rubbed his jaw. "What clues?"

"*X marks the spot* over and over," Chester answered instead of Kate. When Claire gave him a what-the-hell look, he shrugged. "I'm hungry. Jail is no place to spend Thanksgiving. Trust me, I've been there."

Knowing some of what she did about Chester's past with batty women, Claire didn't doubt him for a minute.

"Grady didn't say he was going to throw us in jail." Ronnie sounded as exasperated as Claire felt. "Just take us to the station."

"Close enough," Kate said.

Claire shook her head, looking out to where the damned turkey had stopped to peck at something on the desert floor. At least Ronnie had held her ground, which was surprising considering her intimate relationship with the

Sheriff. Claire wondered how Grady felt about his girlfriend withholding information from him.

"What do you think that means, Claire?" The Sheriff singled her out, surprising her.

She squeezed her lips together, forming her response carefully. As much as being around the cops made her squirmy, she didn't want the Sheriff as an enemy. Cholla County was too small to be playing tag with the law, especially with her older sister sharing a bed with the head honcho.

"Well," she shoved her hands in her back pockets, "I suspect it's a distraction."

"A distraction?" His gaze didn't waver. "Where were these rounds being stored?"

"In Joe's office," Ronnie answered.

Claire glanced at her older sister. Ronnie was being purposely vague.

The Sheriff's radio came to life, a voice ringing through loud and clear, rattling off a string of numbers that sounded like a bingo ball announcement.

The Sheriff listened and then cursed under his breath when the radio returned to silence. "I need to go take care of that." He focused on Claire. "Load them up and get them out of here." His gaze shifted to Ronnie. "I'll catch up with you later."

"Don't forget your Aunt Millie," Ronnie said.

One side of his mouth curled. "Trust me, she isn't letting me." He held out his hand to her. "Walk with me for a moment."

Ronnie looked at his hand for a couple of heartbeats and then took it, leaving Claire to round up the other two and get them back into the clown car, or in this case the jester Jeep.

The inside of the cab smelled sweet and chocolaty with a hint of fruitiness. Claire wondered how long it would take for the milk-based chocolate cream pie to start going sour. She'd fastened her seatbelt and started up the engine by the time Ronnie had returned and climbed inside.

"Everything okay?" Kate asked from the backseat.

"No, Katie, everything is far from okay," Ronnie sounded more tired than angry. "Grady is keeping the derringer for now. He said he'll bring it back later."

"Was that all he had to say?" Claire asked, watching the Sheriff's Bronco do a U-turn and head back to Yuccaville.

"No, there was more."

"Start with the dirty stuff," Chester said. "All of that sugar in the cherry pie is starting to wear off. I don't want to fall asleep before you get to the sex part."

"There is no sex part." Ronnie settled into her seat as Claire rolled out onto the highway. "He knows," she said, staring out the window.

"He knows what?" Kate asked.

"He knows that we're hiding things from him and he warned me that he's not going to put up with games tonight at dinner. He wants answers and is determined to get them from us before the night is over."

Claire shook her head. "This is what happens when the law comes to Thanksgiving."

"You can't blame Grady for this."

"Fine, I'll blame you for inviting him."

"It's Katie's fault, not mine."

"Why is it my fault?" Kate asked, leaning forward. "I'm not the one trying to hide stuff from the Sheriff."

"If you hadn't brought that damned derringer along," Claire started.

"We'd have never found out about another one of Joe's stashes," Kate finished. "You should be thanking me, not blaming me."

Chester laughed. "Who was it that wanted to catch that turkey? Next you'll want us to thank you for a pie-less

Thanksgiving."

"You ate plenty of pie today, Chester Thomas," Kate said, "so you keep your pie-hole shut."

Several bickering-filled minutes later, Claire pulled into the Dancing Winnebago R.V. Park and killed the engine in front of the General Store. She turned and nailed each sister with a glare. "Neither of you is going anywhere until every turkey feather and piece of pie are cleaned up and this Jeep sparkles again."

"It wasn't sparkling when we got in it earlier," Kate pointed out. "I distinctly remember dust on the hood.'

"Just zip it and go get a bucket and some rags."

The screen door creaked open. Claire looked around as Mac came down the porch steps. In his white T-shirt and blue jeans, he looked fresh from the laundry. Not a feather or pie stain on him.

Claire dug some chocolate cream out of the crook of her neck and wiped it on her pants. She tried to tuck her hair behind her ears and wound up with sticky fingers.

"Hey, Slugger," he said, coming around to her window. The breeze ruffled his sandy brown hair. "How was Yucca …" The words died on his tongue as he looked inside the Jeep he'd bought for her as a gift just over a week before.

Claire gave him her best and brightest smile. "How was the drive in from Tucson?"

"Apparently not nearly as exciting as your trip to Yuccaville. What happened? Is that pie? Why are there so many feathers floating around?"

"Ask Crazy Kate."

The back door slammed as the lunatic in the spotlight joined Mac on the outside of the pie-mobile.

Mac took one look at Kate and burst out laughing. When she threatened to hit him with the only pie left—the coconut cream—he raised his hands and swallowed the last of his mirth. "Sorry, Kate. What's with the feathers?"

"I rescued a turkey."

"Then she tried to shoot it with Joe's derringer," Claire added.

Chester joined them. "Then the turkey woke up and went bananas in Claire's new rig, making a mess of the pies the Sheriff's sister made for Thanksgiving."

"And you hogged the cherry," Claire grumbled.

"Then we got pulled over by Grady for multiple offenses," Ronnie said from where she was still sitting inside, her head pressed back against the seat rest.

Kate touched her bloody earlobe gingerly. "The Sheriff threatened to take us to jail again."

"Not jail," Ronnie clarified, "just down to the station."

"And now he's going to interrogate each of us in between passing the mashed potatoes and stuffing," Claire finished with a grimace.

Mac's grin reached each ear. "It sounds like a mash up of *I Love Lucy* and the Three Stooges."

"I don't like your boyfriend right now," Kate told Claire.

That made Mac chuckle. "It's a wonder Grady didn't keel over from laughing when he pulled you over. Wait until Butch hears about this."

Looking at Kate, Claire asked, "You know what I'm thinking?"

Kate opened the coconut cream pie box.

Claire picked up the pie.

"Claire, no!" Mac said.

"You'd look good in coconut, baby," Claire told him as she pretended to take aim.

"Do it, girl." Chester headed toward the porch steps. "It would give a whole new meaning to his nickname, right, Sweet Cheeks?"

As tempted as she was, it was their last pie. Handing it back to Kate, Claire gave Mac a kiss on the lips instead.

"Oh, gag!" Kate said from behind her. "I'm going to go get a bucket and sponge for my eyeballs and your Jeep."

"Weren't you complaining about needing to open The Shaft?" Ronnie hollered out.

"A quick once-over to get the worst of it won't take long." Kate leaned down and pointed in at Ronnie. "Especially with you helping me." She raced up the steps past Chester and disappeared inside the store.

Mac grinned down at Claire. "This pie business is giving me a few ideas for later tonight when we're alone." He leaned over and sniffed her neck. "Is that chocolate?"

"Add a little tequila and refried beans and you'd be following in your mother's footsteps." Chester said from the porch.

Claire recoiled at that memory.

The screen door slammed open.

"Claire!" her grandfather barked. "What's this Katie says about all of the pies being ruined?"

"It's not my fault."

"The coconut is still edible," Chester said.

Gramps made a disgusted sound. "I can't stand coconut pie." His glower deepened. "Please tell me you at least got the fresh turkey."

"Oh, we got it all right." Ronnie finally had climbed out of the Jeep. She rounded the front.

"Where is it?"

"Last I saw it was headed west." Ronnie aimed a crooked grin at Claire. "But we did pick up Chester like the list said."

"And managed to stay out of jail," Claire added.

Chester snorted. "Barely."

"If there's no turkey and one lousy pie, how are we going to have Thanksgiving dinner?" Gramps asked.

"I don't know." Claire followed Mac up the steps, pausing in front of Gramps's red face. "But with the way

Lady Luck has been mooning me today, I have a feeling food is going to be the least of our problems tonight."

Chapter Six

Three hours and a shower later ...

The Shaft was all set up for a Thanksgiving feast, minus a turkey and four out of five pies. When Grady's pickup pulled into the parking lot, Ronnie walked out to meet him and his Aunt Millie.

"Sorry we're a little late," Grady said, lowering the tailgate. "Aunt Millie insisted on stopping at the senior center before leaving Yuccaville."

Ronnie opened the passenger door for his aunt, offering to help her down. Aunt Millie took her up on it, whispering in her ear, "I've got you covered."

That caught Ronnie by surprise. She started to ask what Aunt Millie had meant by that remark, but the old lady shushed her.

"Here you go," Grady said, setting his aunt's walker in front of her. The red dingle balls hanging from the front of it bounced and swayed.

Aunt Millie winked at Ronnie and made a show of using the walker to get her balance. Recently Ronnie had learned that Millie really didn't need a walker. She was playing the part because it offered her more opportunities to pull off her shenanigans.

"Mom's already half-baked," Ronnie told them both, her tone apologetic. "She started hitting the cognac when my father called an hour ago to wish us a Happy Thanksgiving."

Aunt Millie grinned wide. "Sounds like it's gearing up to

be an exciting holiday get together."

"Exciting? More like disastrous."

With a snort, Aunt Millie squeezed Ronnie's arm. "Don't fret, darling. Family dinners without any fireworks are snooze-fests. I took a nap this afternoon so I wouldn't doze off and miss a single moment tonight."

Grady grimaced, pulling down the brim of his cowboy hat. "You promised you'd behave, Aunt Millie."

She jutted her chin at him. "And you promised not to be a spoilsport, boy." She took off across The Shaft's parking lot toward the bar, her walker creaking as she made a show of being feeble.

Grady watched his aunt with a pinched brow. "I have a feeling she has something planned for tonight, and I'll bet it's going to make feathers fly."

"It won't be the first time today."

His gaze lowered, roving over her face and hair, both of which she'd spent a stupid amount of time trying to make look good for him after the pie covered mess she'd been earlier. "You clean up well, Veronica. Did you leave any pie for me to lick off?"

Her pulse leapt. "It was too sticky."

"I like you sticky." He nudged her chin up with his knuckles and gave her a chaste kiss. "And sweet." He ran his thumb over her lower lip. "All afternoon I've been thinking about what you promised to deliver if I came to your family's dinner."

She smiled in spite of what was sure to be a huge Thanksgiving calamity with her mother already firmly on the road to soused-ville. If she could just keep Grady from nosing too deep into the Morgan family secrets tonight, maybe Claire wouldn't follow through on her threat to lock a skunk in their grandpa's R.V. while Ronnie was sleeping.

"You look very handsome today, Sheriff Hardass," she flirted, running her nails down his dark brown shirt. She liked the way the seams emphasized his broad shoulders. His jeans made his legs look long and strong. The cowboy boots and hat gave him a rugged edge that made her feel like a teenage Elvis fan, squealing in her poodle skirt as the King gyrated his hips.

"Handsome enough to wrap you around my pinkie and seduce all of your secrets from those lovely lips?"

She grinned. "Well, you're no god of thunder and lightning."

"What's Thor have that I don't?"

"A very big hammer."

"Have you seen the size of *my* hammer?"

That made her laugh aloud.

Taking her arm, he tucked it in the crook of his elbow and led her to where his Aunt Millie waited outside The Shaft's door. "This is my first Thanksgiving dinner in over five years."

"Don't worry. It's sure to end in an arrest, so you'll feel right at home."

He chuckled. "Does your mother know about us yet?"

"No." She felt his gaze on her. "And there's a very good reason why."

"Let me guess." He stepped ahead to get the door for his aunt. "You're protecting me."

"What's Grady need protection from?" Aunt Millie asked as her nephew opened the door.

"Not what, whom. You'll understand after you meet my mother." Ronnie grimaced at one and then the other. "Just don't look into her eyes."

"Why not?"

"You'll turn into a pillar of salt, of course." Ronnie led the way inside.

Kate couldn't stop thinking about Joe's message.

X marks the spot.

What did that mean? Claire had said it wasn't about a treasure, because Joe never made things as easy as that, but what was easy about that simple and very vague message?

X marks the spot.

What X did he mean? What spot? Was there a map somewhere?

Someone knocked on the door to Butch's office, where Kate had gone to escape their mother's complaining about the lack of turkey on her first Thanksgiving away from home. Claire had tried to convince their mom that it was good to try new things. After all, she was newly married and living in a different state. This mind trick had almost worked until their father had called to wish them all a Happy Thanksgiving and talked about plans for him to come down to Arizona for Christmas.

As good as it was to hear the happiness in his voice after a decade of sourness and angry rants while married to their mom, his coming to Arizona had Claire cursing and Kate chewing on her knuckles.

"Come in," Kate said, bracing for her mother.

Ronnie opened the door. "Grady and his aunt are here."

That meant it was show time. "Did the old bully bring her temper?"

"Don't start, Katie." Ronnie walked over and placed the derringer on Butch's desk. "Grady brought this back. He asked if we'd keep it tucked away in here until everyone is gone."

Kate picked up the palm pistol. "I'll bury it in one of Butch's drawers."

"Butch told me to tell you that Mom's meatloaf surprise is almost done baking."

Unlike their mother, Butch had taken the news about the lack of turkey and pies with a huge grin.

One of the things Kate liked most about the father of her child was his ease dealing with change. Although her announcement about the baby last month had taken a little bit longer for him to swallow after years of planning to never have kids.

Never say never, as the saying goes.

Now he not only accepted his upcoming paternal role, he was building one hell of a nest. Most days, while Kate was just trying to keep her hormones under control, he was either online starting a college fund, trying to decide where to put the swing set, or planning how to incorporate a crib and play area in this very office.

"We've got the tables all pushed together out on the back patio and the places set." Ronnie's voice pulled her back to the present. "Grady's Aunt Millie brought some food, too."

"Why did she do that?"

"A little birdie told her we had some trouble with the pies."

"You mean a six-foot-four rooster who pulled us over and threatened to throw us in jail."

"Grady never actually said *jail*."

"You say tomato," Kate started.

Ronnie interrupted, "And I say get your ass out front and help me keep *your* mother under control." She left Kate with, "Now, Katie!"

Some things never change, especially bossy older sisters.

Kate picked up the derringer. She opened Butch's bottom drawer to put it in and then paused. The shine on the double barrels caught her eye. She turned on Butch's desk lamp and slowly turned the palm pistol underneath it. There were swirling lines going this way and that up the barrels on each side, which she'd noticed earlier waiting outside of Dirty Gerties. But what she hadn't noticed before was how several of them intersected and made little

Xs throughout the pattern. Or were those fancy Vs? She pulled the hammer back and noticed that an X had been carved into the metal over the top of what looked like a cursive P and V.

Did gun owners normally carve letters into their guns? Upon closer inspection, even the P and V appeared to have been added.

X marks the spot.

She carefully set the hammer back in place even though she was positive the pistol was empty. What in the hell did all this mean?

Chapter Seven

"I knew I should've taken that left at Albuquerque," Claire told Mac as she handed him a Tupperware bowl with shredded carrots imprisoned in green gelatin.

"You and Bugs Bunny, Slugger," he said, frowning down at the green disaster. "Those poor carrots deserved better." He handed the bowl to Kate, who sat on his left.

Without a word, she put a spoonful of the green gelatin-covered carrots on her plate and then passed the dish on to Butch.

Kate had been quiet since sitting down at the table. Chester's ribbing about the lack of turkey didn't even light her fuse. Something was up with her, but Claire wasn't in the mood to dig right now. Her main focus was making it through dinner in one piece.

A loud titter from her mother made her wince. A peek her way found Deborah sloshing her cognac while whispering in her husband's ear. While Claire watched, Manny took the glass out of her mom's hand and set it on the table, then put a roll on each of their plates before passing the basket down the line to Gramps.

"Pass the meatloaf," Gramps said to Chester, who held down the seat at the head of the table. Grady was at the opposite end with Ronnie on his left and his aunt on his right.

Chester passed the plate heavy with meat to Claire's grandfather.

In lieu of a real turkey, her mother had made do by

shaping ten pounds of hamburger mixed with bread crumbs and seasoning into the profile of a turkey. It was a fun idea, but unfortunately her culinary masterpiece had been conjured *after* she'd opened her bottle of cognac. Never having been a great sculptor, Deborah's turkey-shaped meatloaf looked more like the eagle on Mexico's flag, especially after Manny added a line of celery sticks end-to-end coming from the bird's beak. The population south of the border would have been proud of the representation of their eagle and serpent; Deborah on the other hand, added more cognac to her glass and cried in her drink about this year's Thanksgiving tragedy.

Besides the meatloaf turkey, side dishes had been supplied from one and all.

Chester brought a saucepan full of *chili con carne* with cheese melted over the top and was currently drowning his meatloaf in the gut-bomb mixture.

Ruby and Gramps made homemade pumpkin rolls, dressing, and mashed potatoes, all of which would make a bellyful of heaven.

Manny and her mother brought a bowl of Manny's famous homemade refried beans with real lard to make them drool-worthy. His corn chips and homemade salsa went great with Butch's beer on tap.

Along with drinks from behind the bar, Butch lined the center of the joined tables with whatever other condiments anyone might want. While Kate stayed put at the table, Butch crisscrossed between the patio and the bar as patrons straggled in for the free meal he offered to those without family or friends to share the holiday.

Before settling in for the meal, Aunt Millie had surprised them all—including her nephew—with covered dishes and Tupperware bowls she'd pulled from her walker's cavernous basket. According to Ronnie, whom the older woman had confided in when the Sheriff had been in the restroom washing his hands, she'd sneaked the food from the senior center on the way to The Shaft. When Ronnie worried aloud about the folks at the center going hungry, Aunt Millie insisted nobody would miss the food because half were too old to eat more than a couple of bites, and the rest would fall asleep before they made it halfway through their pre-dinner salad.

"I've seen it a hundred times," Aunt Millie had told them as she took her place at the table. "Those geezers won't wake from their naps until the workers have cleaned up everything and dumped the leftovers in the trash."

As another casserole dish passed under Claire's nose—this time a colorful mix of orange-colored pudding with purple cabbage in it ... no wait, that looked more like eggplant—Claire was debating on faking a mealtime nap, too. She was about to pass the orange concoction along when Ronnie took the spoon from the bowl and slopped a dollop on Claire's plate. She dumped it right next to the chunk of the meatloaf turkey's right leg that Claire had taken.

At Claire's glare, her sister whispered, "Be nice. Aunt Millie brought it."

"More like stole it," she whispered back, which earned her a pinch on the thigh.

Claire spooned a glob of the orange eggplant pudding onto Mac's plate. When he grimaced down at it, she said, "If it kills me, Romeo, you're drinking the poison, too."

Kate wimped out, claiming she was dealing with some baby-related nausea and passed the dish over Butch's plate, which sat waiting for him to return from another check on his patrons.

Chester took it from her, sniffed the orange pudding, shrugged, and plopped several spoons' worth on his plate next to his mound of *chili con carne*. Claire needed to remind him and Manny not to light up cigars within twenty feet of the old Winnebago Brave. That poor camper would probably have the wallpaper peeling off when Chester started off-gassing.

Aunt Millie's other stolen food donations included a bowl of watery tapioca pudding ruined with a mixture of raisins and prunes floating among the white tapioca pearls; a dish of stale fruitcake slices that Claire suspected was left over from last Christmas after Manny almost chipped a tooth on his first nibble; and a plate stacked high with soft and delicious rice crispy squares. Millie claimed those were her own. If all else failed on the food front, Claire planned on slipping away to the bathroom with the plate of marshmallow goodies.

Mac had brought her favorite cranberry relish from a Tucson deli close to his house along with a six-pack of his cousin's favorite grape soda. Jessica had squealed in delight at the sugar filled soda, and that was before gulping down a can of it.

Grady had begged two more pies from his sister. He swore to Ronnie that he hadn't said a word to her about the wild turkey situation and claimed his sister had generously given up a cherry and an apple pie that she'd made for the rest of Grady's family when he'd mentioned they needed a few more for The Shaft.

While Ronnie had worried her lip about the extra pies, Claire had elbowed her and mouthed, *Let it go!* Claire wanted to eat some cherry pie that had not come from Chester's lap.

When Ronnie had thanked Grady for his thoughtfulness, he'd winked at her and pulled four cans of whipped cream topping out of a grocery bag, claiming they were for the pies. However, Claire hadn't missed the heated look he'd shot her sister. Nor had she missed Ronnie's instantly flushed cheeks, or that one can of whipped cream mysteriously disappeared by the time the dessert table had been set up over on the side of the patio.

Claire prayed that she didn't walk in on that whipped cream rendezvous like she had with her mother. A lifetime worth of therapy wouldn't even dent the tanker-sized sordid memory now beached in her brain for all eternity.

After filling the rest of her plate with Ruby's mashed potatoes, rolls, and dressing, along with a large portion of cranberry relish to coat her mom's meatloaf, Claire dug in. She started with Ruby's food and had made it halfway through her plate when Kate started coughing in the midst of eating some green Jell-O.

Covering her mouth with her napkin, Kate spit something into it. When she peeked into the cloth, her face turned ashen. "I think I just choked on a toenail."

"Kathryn Lynette." Deborah set down her glass of cognac. "Stop being so melodramatic and eat."

Oh, she was one to talk after all of those tears in her meatloaf.

"I'm serious." Kate held her napkin out for all to see. "Look."

Sure enough, a crescent moon of a toenail lay amidst a green stained background on the napkin.

"Son of a gun," Aunt Millie said. "I must have grabbed one of Esther's dishes. That old gal gets mixed up sometimes."

"And puts her toenails in Jell-O?" Mac asked in disbelief, a grimace lining his face.

"Yup. She thinks she's a witch. Last year at Christmas, she sprinkled dehydrated centipedes over her green bean casserole in place of dried onions. There was no mistaking all of those little legs."

"Dios mio!" Manny stared down at his spoon of tapioca pudding. He poked a prune a couple of times.

"Oh, don't worry about the tapioca pudding. That's clean. Gloria wins blue ribbons at the county fair for her pudding every year." Aunt Millie pointed her fork at the small pile of green gelatin on his plate. "I'd skip the green stuff if I were you, though. Esther usually includes fly wings in any dish with toenails."

Kate made a gagging sound and scrubbed her tongue with her napkin.

Before returning to her cranberry relish, Claire noticed that everyone was inspecting each bite of food before sticking it into their mouths. All except Chester, who was shoveling it in as fast as his spoon could deliver.

Several moments later, Gramps coughed in the midst of eating a slice of meatloaf.

"What is it?" Kate asked, her fork frozen midair, her eyes wide. "Was there something in the meatloaf?"

"No, it's just dry as hell." He reached for his glass of beer. "What did you use in place of bread crumbs?" he asked Deborah.

"What do you mean what did I use, Dad? I used the bread crumbs that were in that old peanut butter jar in the cupboard."

Ruby lowered her fork, her eyes wide. "I don't have a jar full of bread crumbs."

After a belch into his closed fist, Chester spoke up. "Are you talking about that jar full of sawdust I put on the top shelf of Ruby's cupboard?"

Deborah's face blanched. "Oh no." She reached for her glass of cognac.

"Chester Thomas!" Ruby exclaimed in her soft Oklahoma accent. "Why on earth would ya put a jar of sawdust in my cupboard?"

"I needed a place to store it when we were remodeling your rec room." He grabbed a dinner roll and pointed it at Claire. "It's her fault."

"What? How is it my fault?"

"You went on that cleaning frenzy, all fired up about

spit-shining the place before Mac came for the weekend. I didn't want you to throw out my jar of saw dust, so I stuffed it up in the cupboard. Figured I'd get it later."

"That doesn't make this my fault."

"You distracted me with that story about Katie locking Deputy Dipshit in his own jail cell. I would've remembered I'd put it up there otherwise."

"I put sawdust in the meatloaf," Deborah whined to Manny. "First Dad's dog ruined the turkey I was brining and then my own daughter sabotages my meatloaf."

Great! Claire blew out a sigh. Now Deborah had another life tragedy to blame on her least favorite child. "There was no sabotaging involved, Mom."

Chester took a bite out of a roll. "If you wouldn't have had your nose buried in the bottle," he said through a mouthful of bread, "you would've been able to smell that it was sawdust and not bread crumbs."

"Let me get something straight," Grady's commanding voice silenced the squabbling. He eyeballed each of them in turn from his seat at the end of the table. "Kate was the one who locked my deputy in the holding cell?"

In the silence that followed his question, the plastic beer flags hanging overhead flapped in the light breeze.

A semi-tractor trailer rolled by out front.

Chester's spoon scraped over his plate.

The patio door slid open and Butch stepped out. He sat down next to Kate, dropped his napkin on his lap, and grabbed a pumpkin roll. "What did I miss?"

Jessica giggled, setting her can of grape pop down. "You missed toenails in the Jell-O, sawdust in the meatloaf, and Kate locking the Sheriff's deputy in his own jail cell."

"Huh." Butch placed his napkin back on the table and scooted his chair back. "I forgot something in the kitchen."

He started to stand, but Kate grabbed his arm and tugged him down into his seat. "Oh, no you don't. Escaping is not an option, Valentine Carter."

"Thanksgiving is ruined!" Deborah cried with a healthy dose of Shakespearean tragedy in her tone. She took center stage again, picking up her butter knife and holding it out threateningly toward Chester. "And it's all your fault!"

Manny took the butter knife from her hand and laid it on the table out of her reach. "*Mi amor*, this is not a big deal. There is plenty of food to eat at this table." He forked off a bite of meatloaf and chewed on it, then swallowed with a slight grimace. "That piece tasted perfect," he said. "Plus, it has extra fiber in every bite." He grabbed his beer and took a long swig.

Meanwhile, at the other end of the table, the Sheriff sat back in his chair, his arms crossed over his chest. "How many of you knew about the trick Kate pulled on my deputy?"

Kate and Ronnie both turned to Claire as if she were the kingpin in the lock-up-Deputy-Dipshit plot. "Why are you two looking at me? I was working at The Shaft that night."

"I knew about it," Chester said, shoveling a big spoonful of mashed potatoes into his even bigger mouth. "And I told Manny about it."

Gramps bristled. "How come you two didn't tell me?"

"Because you were horsing around up in South Dakota at the time," Chester said.

"She's your granddaughter," Manny added. "We didn't want you being too hard on her for having a little fun."

"Yeah, well she's your stepdaughter now, and you need to get her under control."

"Kathryn is not my responsibility," Manny said. "She's Butch's."

Kate pushed to her feet, puffed up and sputtering. "Listen, you two, I'm the one responsible for me, got it?"

"Got it," the Sheriff cut in, his expression rigid. It

turned out he could be just as intimidating without his badge and sunglasses. "So, Kate," his eyes narrowed, "why don't you tell me all about the joke you played on my deputy?"

Ronnie made sit-down motions to Kate.

She deflated back down to her seat. "Uh, Butch, didn't you say you told the Sheriff about how Carter babies make women do things they don't normally do?"

Chuckling, Butch leaned over to kiss her forehead. "I sure did, sweetheart."

"So," Sheriff Harrison raised his brows. "Let me get this straight. You're claiming temporary insanity as your excuse for sneaking into my station, shutting down the security cameras, and locking my deputy in a jail cell while he was on duty?"

"Didn't she throw his cellphone in the toilet, too?" Chester mumbled around a bite of pumpkin roll.

As Kate sat squirming, Deborah broke the silence with a loud cackle of laughter. "Whose idea was it to bring the cops to our party?" She raised her glass to Grady, slurring even more than she had minutes before. "What's next, lawman? You gonna arrest me for public intoxication? Or how about this?" she grabbed Manny and gave him a loud wet kiss in front of everyone, making groans roll around the table like a stadium wave. When she pulled back, she glared at Grady. "Public display of affection, Mr. Big-time Sheriff."

Something was wrong with this picture. Deborah was either suddenly very drunk, which didn't match how much cognac was still in her glass, or she was overacting for some reason. As Deborah gave the Sheriff her infamous testicle-shriveling glare-down, Claire could feel the tension in the air doubling and tripling. She shot her oldest sister a *do something* look.

Ronnie's forehead wrinkled. She glanced from Claire to

their mom to Grady, and then nodded to herself.

"I have an announcement to make," Ronnie declared, standing.

All eyes turned to her.

She licked her lips. "Grady and I are … uh … going steady."

"Going steady?" Claire repeated. That was the best Ronnie could come up with as a distraction?

"What do you mean going steady?" Deborah asked, the slur gone from her voice.

"She means riding the dragon upon St. George," Chester answered and then took a swig from a can of the cheap beer he'd bought earlier at the store.

Claire—and everyone else at the table—paused to frown at the old goat.

"What's riding the dragon upon St. George mean?" Jessica asked her mother.

Ruby shot a frown in Chester's direction.

Aunt Millie let out a cackle of laughter. "I haven't heard that saying since I was back in college."

Claire hadn't heard it ever.

"I once messed around a time or two with an art history major," Chester explained, spooning more dressing onto his plate. "That was her code word for …" he glanced at Jessica, who was leaning forward, eager to learn. "For having inverted relations."

Inverted? Boy, did that paint several pictures in Claire's head, none of which were pretty or appropriate for a Thanksgiving dinner table.

Deborah stood, her cheeks mottled. "Veronica, you're having inverted relations with *him*?" Their mother pointed a sharp-tipped, pink fingernail at Grady, who looked more pained than kingly all of a sudden. "The Sheriff of Cholla County?"

Ronnie held steady against their mother's gale force

glare. "Yes, I am."

"Why?" Deborah made that one word sound as if Ronnie had stabbed her in the heart. "You know your sisters' penchant for crime."

Aunt Millie laughed again. "I love this family," she told her nephew.

"Now hold on a second," Claire joined the standing ranks. "I do not have a penchant for crime."

Mac chuckled. When she glared down at him, he covered his mouth with his napkin and looked away.

"You do tend to lie low around the law," Kate said. At Claire's huff, she said, "What? That's not an official crime. It's just sort of criminal acting."

"Thanks for having my back, knucklehead." Claire focused back on Deborah. "If you'll remember, Kate's the one who always dated criminals."

"Not always." When Butch cleared his throat, Kate smiled at him. "They were just petty criminals, charged with misdemeanors most of the time."

"And," Claire continued, "she's the reason I've landed in jail the last four times."

"Only three were because of me," Kate corrected.

"None of this matters, Mother," Ronnie interrupted. "Neither does Grady's profession as a lawman."

Several scoffs echoed around the table, including one from Claire. Grady was a good guy, but she had a feeling his badge was going to cause some friction, at the very least give her blisters.

"Woo-wee!" Aunt Millie's grin split wide as she looked at her nephew. "Sort of feels like you landed in a pit of rattlers here." She grabbed the dish of cranberry relish. "You better tuck in, boy, and start toe-stepping, or you'll end up taking a dirt nap out back of that Winnebago park with a cross over your head like the others."

Huh. How did Aunt Millie know about the old graves

back in the dry gulch behind the Dancing Winnebago R.V. Park?

"A cross over your head," Kate repeated, her forehead tightening as she stared down at her plate.

"Mrs. Morgan," Grady started to address their mother. "I can assure you—"

"It's Mrs. Carrera, Sheriff," Deborah corrected. Outlaws looked less hostile than their mother at the moment.

"Don't look in her eyes," Ronnie whispered.

"Oh, hell," Mac said under his breath. "I know that stare. Keep your head down, Slugger."

"I don't get it, Veronica." Their mother's focus returned to Ronnie. "After the mess we're still dealing with because of your ex's crimes, you're once again putting your family at risk. For what?"

"Mom, don't. The Sheriff is a nice guy." Claire tried to derail the train before it ended in a smoking heap of twisted wreckage. "He means well."

"Shut up, Claire," Deborah said without taking her eyes off Ronnie. "If the Sheriff meant well, I would *not* be learning about his interest in my oldest daughter *after* he got free milk from the cow."

Aunt Millie cackled again. "This just keeps getting better."

"A cross over his head," Kate said again, louder. She stood up so fast her chair nearly fell over backwards. "Sheriff Harrison, I need to see your gun!"

Chapter Eight

"I'd like to take a timeout from this fun game of the Sheriff's Dungeons and St. George's Dragons to deal with Kate's temporary loss of sanity," Claire said.

"I'm serious," Kate said. "I think I figured it out."

"If you're talking about how to put your mom out of our misery," Chester said, returning from the dessert table with a piece of cherry pie and a stack of rice crispy squares. "I already suggested shooting her, but Ford and Carrera weren't up for it."

"Not Mom. I mean *X marks the spot.*"

"You're still stuck on that?" Ronnie asked.

Claire should have known Kate wouldn't let that go for now. "I think she's carrying a miniature Sherlock Holmes in her uterus."

Groaning, Mac laid down his fork. "I vote we not discuss Kate's uterus at the dinner table."

"That's better than talking about the muscles in her birth canal and the elasticity of her vagina," Jessica said.

More groans echoed around the table.

"Jessica Lynn!" Ruby hit her daughter with a stern scowl. "How many times do I need to tell you to keep what you're learnin' in health class to yourself?"

"Make up your mind!" Jessica pouted down at her plate. "First you say you want to know what I'm learning in sex ed, and then you tell me I can't talk about it."

"There is a time and place, child. Neither is fixin' to be now or here."

"Sheriff," Kate started. "If you'll just let me look at your gun for a moment."

"Of course," Grady said with a straight face. "But first let me take off the safety so you can shoot a hole in something else today."

"I'd aim it at Deborah's ass," Chester said, taking a bite out of a marshmallow square. He snickered when their mother threw her napkin at him.

"You shot a gun today, Kate?" Butch asked, his pitch higher than normal.

"Just a tiny one."

"You're pregnant!"

"Newsflash, Valentine—being with child does not render my shooting finger immobile."

"What were you shooting at?"

"It wasn't on purpose." Her forehead turned pink. Kate had never been able to blush like a normal person ... nor shoot, apparently. "I accidentally shot Claire's Jeep."

"She shot a hole in your new Jeep?" Mac gaped at Claire. "Christ, you barely had it two weeks before she tried to kill it."

"I said it was an accident, Mac," Kate said, pinching his bicep. "Grady, I promise not to pull the trigger. Can I please just take a peek at your gun?"

Grady shook his head, a grin on his lips. "No way, Crash Morgan." His use of the nickname he'd given her after she'd crunched Butch's truck the second time made Kate's forehead burn even redder. "That would go directly against my oath to serve and protect."

"Why do you need Grady's gun, Katie?" Ronnie lowered herself into her seat. "What does that have to do with X *marks the spot*?"

"What in the hell is this X *marks the spot* business?" Gramps asked.

Claire hesitated, looking at Ruby. She didn't like to talk

about Joe and his criminal past in front of Ruby if she could help it. The poor woman beat herself up enough on her own for marrying the asshole who'd left her with a passel of stolen goods and a heap of debt.

"If you're fixin' to tell me this is about Joe," Ruby said, "I won't be surprised one bit."

Before Claire could decide if spilling the beans in front of mixed company was a good idea, Ronnie beat her to it. She kept her explanation brief, though, leaving out a few details after a conspiratorial glance at Claire.

"Oooh," Jessica said, rubbing her hands together. "I hope there's a chest full of gold buried somewhere."

Ruby smirked. "More like a chest full of stolen trouble, if you ask me."

"Who gave you the combination to the basement safe?" Gramps asked Kate.

She studied her fingernails. "I sort of overheard it."

"Have you guys put anything else in the safe lately?" Jessica asked. The teenager had been on scene with Claire the day she'd first figured out the combination. When it came to things that could possibly benefit her, such as treasures that might finance her newest want—a car—Jess had a photographic memory.

"None of your business," Gramps and Ruby said in unison.

"Kathryn," Manny said, draping his arm over the back of his wife's seat. "Why do you need to see the Sheriff's Glock?"

"Because I think there's something different about that derringer from other guns."

"You're right," Grady said. "First of all, that derringer is an antique."

"I'm not talking about the age of it," Kate said. "I noticed something different on the gun itself."

"What?"

"There are some markings on the hammer. If you let me see your gun, I'll show you where."

"My Glock doesn't have a hammer. My Colt 45 does, but that's at home."

"Damn."

The Sheriff raised one black eyebrow. "Are you talking about the P and the V with the X scratched over them?"

Kate's face lit up. "Yes! What does that mean?"

"That it's stolen."

All eyes turned to him.

"From what I could figure out this afternoon, I believe it belongs in a museum in El Paso that has a collection of Pancho Villa's personal effects, including his firearms."

"Bull-pucky," Aunt Millie said.

Grady continued: "Several items were reported stolen according to a police case that was opened almost ten years ago. One of the items was a pearl handled derringer. I'll need to dig a little more to find a picture of it for comparison."

"That pea shooter belonged to Pancho Villa?" Chester lowered his forkful of cherry pie. "I thought Villa liked rifles—Mauser carbines and Winchesters."

"*Sí,*" Manny said, "but a Bisley Colt with mother-of-pearl handles was his one true *amor.*"

"A Bisley Colt is a far cry from that dainty little palm pistol."

"Maybe he got it for one of his women," Kate said.

"You're telling me that Kate shot a hole in my Jeep with a gun that once belonged to Pancho Villa?" Claire shook her head. Thank God Joe hadn't stolen a Tommy gun from an Al Capone collection and left it lying around for Kate to find.

Mac leaned forward, catching Grady's eye. "Did Villa have his initials on any other guns in the collection?"

"Nothing was mentioned in the report I read, but it wasn't the initials that tipped me off, it was the inscription written in Spanish on the underside of the barrels."

"I must have missed that," Kate said.

"It's pretty small and partially worn off, plus it looks like part of the design," Grady told her. "I didn't see it at first either, but it's mentioned in the description on the report the museum filed. Once I got out a magnifying glass, it was mostly legible."

Ronnie touched Grady's arm, drawing his gaze. "What's it say?"

"*Viva México?*" Manny asked.

Grady shook his head. "*Viva los Dorados!*"

"Ahhh," Manny said nodding.

"What are *los Dorados*?" Deborah asked.

"The Golden Ones—they were Villa's personal guard." Manny explained.

"His elite fighting force," Grady added.

"Pancho Villa, huh?" Claire asked, thinking about how Joe's clues often worked. "What did you say the name of his favorite pistol was?"

"A Bisley Colt," Chester said, scraping his plate clean. He looked up at her and did a double take. "Why do you have that look on your face, girl?"

"What look?"

Mac grinned. "The one that says you've locked your teeth onto something."

"Claire," Kate pushed Mac back to see her better. "What is it?"

"X marks the spot."

"Yeah?"

"You know those old graves I showed you way back in the dry gulch that extends behind the R.V. park?"

"Yeah?"

"Remember the grave with the crooked cross? The one with the name carved into the wood?"

Kate gasped. "Bisley!" She clapped. "Ha! I knew it! All through dinner I kept seeing a crooked X in my head, trying to make sense of it. It must have been that old cross."

Claire turned to Mac. "We have to go dig up that grave."

"Right now?"

"Of course right now. The sun will be setting soon."

"If there is anything buried back there, it's not going to go anywhere before morning."

Kate looked at Mac as if he'd grown two heads. "You'd be able to sleep tonight without knowing what's buried there?"

"Mac can sleep through anything," Claire said.

Kate tossed her napkin on the table. "Claire, you drive and I'll dig."

"You're not digging, Katie, you're pregnant," Ronnie said. "I'll dig."

"Hold it right there!" Grady said in his sheriff's voice, freezing everyone in their places. "Nobody is digging up any graves in my county." He pushed away his plate of uneaten sawdust meatloaf and green toenail gelatin, his narrowed gaze moving around the table until they landed on Ronnie. "At least not until I get a piece of pie." A smile rounded the corners of his mouth. "And a little whipped cream."

Ronnie licked her lips. "Just a little?"

Wanting to get out to that grave, Claire volunteered to dish up dessert for everyone.

Deborah joined her, playing pie delivery girl. "So, your sister has managed to hook the county sheriff," Deborah said quietly to Claire.

"Yep." Claire finished slicing the coconut pie into eight pieces before moving on to the other two. She set two pieces of cherry aside for her and Mac. "Whether it's good or bad for the rest of us remains to be seen, but he seems to really like Ronnie." Not to mention that he's a smart ally to have if someone else came gunning for her sister.

"How'd you like my distraction?" Deborah asked when Claire handed her a plate of coconut pie to take to the dinner table.

"What do you mean?"

"I got him to stop focusing on Kate locking up his deputy pretty quickly there, don't you think?"

Claire pulled back in surprise. "You mean you're not really mad at Ronnie for hooking up with Grady?"

Deborah shrugged. "I worry that she's rebounding. But I'm learning that you girls are going to live your own lives no matter how I carry on about your choices."

"Is that the cognac talking?"

"Maybe a little, but Manny's been working on me, too. You girls have quite an advocate in your new stepfather."

Claire smiled as her mother walked away. Another Thanksgiving dinner was almost wrapped up. Disaster had been narrowly averted several times during the meal and they'd live to see another day.

"What are you smiling about, Slugger?" Mac came up beside her and wrapped his arm around her shoulder, dropping a kiss on her temple.

"Our family."

"They're all nuts, you know."

"Yeah. They sure are." She shoved a piece of cherry pie at him, spritzing the top with whipped cream. "Now hurry up and eat. We have some grave digging to do."

Chapter Nine

By the time they made it to the R.V. park, it was well past dark o'clock. Claire and her flashlight led the way back into the dry gulch beyond the park's fence line. She knew the lay of the land better than anyone else in their grave digging crew.

Chester, Manny, Deborah, Gramps, Ruby, and Aunt Millie had all stayed back at Ruby's place, enjoying some games of Euchre in the warm, well-lit rec room. Jessica had shown an interest in coming along until she found out digging would be involved and figured they'd make her do most of the work since she was the youngest. Claire didn't steer the kid's speculation in any different direction. She'd rather Jessica not be there to squeal at any weird noises coming from the surrounding scrub brush or see what—if anything—they pulled out of the ground.

"How much further?" Kate asked.

Claire had tried to talk her pregnant sister out of coming along, but the nutso had insisted. After all, she'd claimed, if it weren't for her wanting to rescue the wild turkey they wouldn't be going on a treasure hunt tonight. When Butch had heard Kate's plans, he'd closed up the bar and joined them rather than try to talk sense into her.

"Why?" Claire glanced back at Kate. "Are you getting nervous?"

"No, these boots are killing me."

"I told you to go home and get your sneakers."

"There was no time. I know you too well. You wouldn't

have waited for me."

Kate was right. Claire was tired of waiting for everyone else. The more she thought about Joe and his history, the more curious she got about what they might dig up.

If anything, a doubt-filled voice said in her head.

"Don't get your hopes too high," she warned Kate. "This could be another one of Joe's wild goose chases."

"And how does that compare to a Morgan sisters' wild turkey chase?" Grady asked from the back of the group.

Claire grinned, enjoying the Sheriff a lot more when he was joking rather than threatening jail time. "There's less pie involved."

"I'm hoping for less gunplay, too," he shot back.

"Ronnie," Claire called over her shoulder as she stepped around a prickly pear cactus. "Remind me to sic Mom on your going-steady partner again when we get back to Ruby's."

Grady's groan echoed off the steep walls. Or maybe the sound came from Mac and Butch groaning in agreement.

They trekked through the narrowing gulch for another ten minutes, dodging more prickly pear and cholla cacti. The moon was down to a sliver. Full stomachs from dinner and pie slowed their progress.

As they neared the bend where the old grave marker had been driven into the desert floor at the base of the wall, Claire heard a rattling sound coming from the brush up ahead.

Something huffed at her.

She paused and sniffed, picking up traces of a pungent, musky scent.

"Javelina," Mac said, drawing up next to her. He shined his beam around the scrub brush and cacti. "Over there."

"I count fourteen," Butch joined them.

"Oh, look!" Kate pointed her light in the direction of the herd. "There are two babies. Aren't they cute?"

One of the larger ones huffed at them again.

"Where's the grave marker?" Grady asked when he and Ronnie caught up.

"Over where those javelinas are hanging out." Claire searched the desert floor with her flashlight. "There, see it?"

Mac stepped toward the herd and clapped his hands several times. The javelinas darted this way and that, then turned and scuttled further back into the gulch. When the last one was gone, Mac led the way to the wooden marker.

"*X marks the spot*," Ronnie said as they stood around it. She sounded like her nose was stuffed up.

Claire shined the light on her. "Why are you plugging your nose?"

"Those javelinas are smelly."

"They're not that bad," Claire said.

"Your sense of smell has sucked ever since you got sprayed by that skunk," Kate said and then giggled. "You stunk for days after that."

Having been at ground zero when the skunk had lifted its tail, there hadn't been much Claire could do at the time besides bawl like a cow stuck in the mud. "Not all of us can smell like roses all of the time, brat."

"You always smell like roses to me, Slugger." Mac patted her on the butt and then hefted the shovel he'd brought along. "How about we see what sort of loot ol' Captain Joe buried before Long John Silver gets here and tries to steal it out from under us."

Shovel at the ready, he waved Butch over, who was carrying Ruby's pickax. Together the two of them dug into the hard desert soil under the crooked grave marker. After several minutes, Grady took a turn swinging the pickax, giving Butch a rest.

Claire offered to help, which earned her three male scoffs in response. "Hey, I do this kind of hard work every day while you pretty boys are keeping your fingernails clean."

"Damned woman," Grady said with a crooked smile, leaning on the pickax. "This early in the dig and you're already insulting our manhood." He shook his head at Mac. "She's been taking notes from her older sister."

"She learned from the best," Ronnie told him and then dodged his hand, putting Kate between them as he reached for her.

"For ground that was supposedly dug up before," Mac said switching the shovel for the pickax, "this is some hard-ass *caliche*." He slammed the pickax into the dirt barely making a dent.

"We need a widow-maker," Claire said, wishing she'd thought to bring the pointed, heavy pole along with them.

"I already have a pregnant one right here," Butch joked, thumbing in Kate's direction. That earned him a sock to the shoulder from his baby momma.

"What's *caliche*?" Ronnie asked.

"It's a sedimentary rock that's been hardened into a sort of natural cement with …" Claire paused. "What's the stuff that binds with other materials in *caliche*, Mac?"

"Calcium …" he swung again, "… carbonate."

"Forget the widow-maker," Grady said with a grunt, using the shovel's head to try to chop down through the *caliche*. "We need a backhoe."

"Whenever you boys need me to step in and take over," Claire crossed her arms, taking one of the Sheriff's favorite stances, "just give a holler. I'll show you how it's done."

Mac shucked his jacket. "Keep it up, Slugger, and I may take you up on it." He tossed his jacket at her to hold. "You do have one hell of a swing." His gaze lowered to her hips, his smile cocky, and then he returned to his own swing.

Lots of sweating and cursing later, they were still coming up empty. The guys stood back, taking a breather.

Claire shined her flashlight into the knee-deep hole.

"There's nothing here." Damn it, Joe had fooled her again.

"Maybe they just need to dig deeper," Kate said.

"No, this is too easy." Claire rubbed her forehead.

Mac coughed. "Easy, she says."

"Joe never makes things so simple," she continued.

"You almost sound like you respect him," Ronnie said, joining her at the empty hole.

"Respect? No. But I do enjoy a challenge." She shined the light on the grave marker with BISLEY carved into it, wondering what Joe had been thinking when he set this up. "And Joe rarely lets me down."

Kate picked up the grave marker. "If it's not here, why did he name this grave after Pancho Villa's favorite gun?"

"Maybe it wasn't Joe who made the marker." Butch took the wooden cross from Kate. "Maybe it was whoever owned the park before Joe."

"X marks the spot," Claire whispered, shining her flashlight on the two other wooden crosses. Neither had any name carved into them. Was the BISLEY grave a red herring?

She pointed her flashlight back at the hole. The *caliche* ran deep. They were already a few feet down and there was no end in sight. Mac was right—the ground hadn't been dug up any time in recent history.

Mac came up next to her, staring down into the shallow dent they'd made in the rock-hard desert floor. "You don't think he was making a play on *The Good, The Bad, and The Ugly*, do you?"

"There are no UNKNOWN marked graves." Grady said what Claire had been thinking.

She replayed the end of that movie in her head, remembering how Tuco had run around and around the huge graveyard. "I don't think so, Blondie," Claire said to Mac, using Clint Eastwood's nickname from the movie.

Ronnie's teeth started to chatter. "I'm freezing my ass

off back here. How about we figure this out when the sun is shining?"

"I told you to grab Mom's leather coat."

"No way, not after you found a condom in the pocket of her other jacket. I'd rather get frostbite."

"You're not going to get frostbite in the Sonoran desert, spaz."

"X marks the spot," Kate said in a disgruntled tone. She was festering again. "I don't like Joe's games."

"I don't like his crimes," Grady said, handing Ronnie the flannel jacket he'd taken off earlier when he'd been digging. "Here, use this to keep warm."

The jacket was huge on her, making her look like a little girl. After sniffing the collar, she shot Grady a flirty smile. "Thanks, Sheriff Hardass."

"What do you say, Slugger?" Mac kicked at the chunks of *caliche*-cemented dirt they'd piled next to the hole. "Keep digging or try again later?"

Claire shined her light in a circle around the gulch, glancing up the tall dirt walls. Ghostly scrub bushes shivered in the cold breeze, their thorny barren branches scratching at the hardpan soil. A tumbleweed rocked back and forth, caught on a prickly pear cactus. A strong gust whipped through the mini canyon. The NO TRESPASSING sign quivered as the wind whistled through the bullet holes peppering it. A plastic bag stuck on a piece of barbed wire fence half buried in one of the walls rustled in rhythm with the wind's periodic drafts.

Claire pulled her jean jacket tight at her throat, trying to keep the cold breeze from reaching down inside her collar. Maybe she should have grabbed her mom's coat. "I suppose we can head back to—"

Wait a second!

She hit the NO TRESSPASSING sign again with her beam of light.

Kate moved beside her. "What do you see?"

"Look at the pattern of the bullet holes."

Her sister gasped. "X marks the spot."

"Sheriff," Claire said, "could a derringer with .22 caliber rounds make those holes?"

"Sure."

"Mac," she started.

"I'm already on it, Slugger." He crossed the gulch and thrust his shovel blade into the sandy soil at the base of the sign. Butch took the pickax from Grady and joined him.

The desert floor was much softer here, mostly sand left behind from storm runoff. Butch didn't have to swing the pickax even once, so he took a turn with the shovel instead. Almost four feet down, the shovel blade hit something metal, and it wasn't the sign post.

They all huddled around Butch, watching as Grady lowered himself to his knees and reached down into the hole to brush off what looked like an old ammo box. Words were stenciled on the top.

"What's it say?" Ronnie asked.

Claire handed Grady her flashlight.

He dusted the lid more. "250 Rounds," he read. "And then it lists a 'Lot' number." He blew at the dirt. "The rest of it is scratched off."

"Grady, you lift while I leverage it," Butch said, wedging the shovel blade under the edge of the box. "Ready?"

Grady nodded.

"Watch your fingers." Butch put his weight onto the handle. "Holy shit, this is heavy."

Mac got down next to Grady. While Butch worked the shovel, the other two hauled out the metal box with a lot of grunting and swearing. The size of it reminded Claire of her grandfather's old Army footlocker, only a little more square than rectangular.

Kate shined her light on the padlock that sealed the box shut. "Grady, give me your gun."

The Sheriff laughed. "For the second time tonight, Crash Morgan, that isn't going to happen."

"Stand back," Butch said. He stepped between Kate and the box. A couple of well-placed strikes with the shovel blade and the lock was history.

"Well," Mac said, looking at Claire. "Who wants to have the honor of opening it?"

Everyone else followed his lead, turning to Claire.

"I say we let Crazy Kate do it," she said, putting her arm around her little sister's shoulders. "After all, she's the one who started it all by packing heat on our trip to Yuccaville this morning."

Kate didn't hesitate. She reached for the shovel handle.

"What are you doing?" Claire asked.

"You don't think I'm dumb enough to open that with my bare hands, do you?" She handed Claire her flashlight.

"What do you think is in there? A bunch of scorpions?"

"I'm not taking any chances." She unhooked the clasp and then used the shovel to lift the lid and flip it open.

Claire and Ronnie both shined their lights inside. Mac cursed under his breath while Butch let out a low whistle and Grady groaned.

"Are those what I think they are?" Ronnie whispered.

"If you mean large bars of silver," Claire replied, "then yes."

"I had no idea they could be so big," Kate said, reaching out to touch one. "They're as big as a bread loaf pan."

Claire crossed her arms over her chest, frowning at Mac. "Who do you think Joe stole these from?"

"Someone who is undoubtedly missing them." Mac looked across at Butch. "Are the numbers on them troy ounces or some sort of numerical identifier?"

"Both is my guess." Butch said. "Grady, I suppose you're going to tell me these came from Pancho Villa, too."

Grady reached into the box and lifted one of the solid silver bars with both hands. "Damn, they're heavy."

"If they're .999 pure silver bullion," Mac said, "they should be close to seventy pounds each."

He would know with all of those geology classes he had in college, Claire thought with a smirk.

Grady lowered the silver bar back into the box after nobody else showed an interest in holding it.

"You know," Grady said to Butch, "you may have something with that Pancho Villa idea. Villa stole 122 silver bars from a train heading north out of Mexico back in the early 1900s."

"You mean the infamous train robbery of 1913?" Claire asked. What were the chances of these three bars being part of the 122 that Villa and his men had stolen?

Grady tipped his hat back and stared up at her, his brow arched in surprise. "You know your Southwest history."

"Claire has taken more college classes than all of us put together, probably," Ronnie explained.

"I thought the story of missing silver bars was fake," Mac said. "A tall tale to keep treasure hunters busy."

"Seems like I read something a while back that only 93 bars were returned," Grady told him. "Villa claimed the rest of the bars were taken by his men, and he didn't know their location."

"Is there a way to tell if they are part of the Villa train robbery?" Claire asked.

Grady shrugged. "I can research the robbery and see if I can find a copy of the original manifest listing the numbered bars. If my memory serves me right, the silver belonged to various mines down in Mexico, but I'm not sure if they were owned by American or Mexican mining companies."

They all stared down at the three silver bars.

"So what do we do with these for now?" Ronnie asked.

"We could bury them again for safekeeping," Claire suggested, not wanting whoever might come looking for them to find them too close to the R.V. park.

"I could store them in evidence," Grady offered.

"But then your deputies will have access to them," Kate returned, her tone clear on how she felt about his deputies.

"I could keep them in my safe for now," Butch said.

Ronnie frowned at him. "You mean that small one in your office at The Shaft?"

"No. The one built into my basement wall at home."

"He does have the best security system around," Grady said.

Mac chuckled. "Kate and Claire can vouch for that." His reference to the time they got busted for sneaking around Butch's place, ending up in jail, earned him a playful slap from both sisters. He laughed even more.

"I vote for Butch's safe," Kate said. "These won't fit in the wall safe in Ruby's basement."

Nor did Claire want them there. "I second that. All in favor?"

They all raised their hands.

"Great." Mac looked at Butch and then Grady. "Now who's going to cart this heavy sucker all of the way back to the campground?"

"What do you say, Veronica?" Grady asked, standing and tugging Ronnie toward him by one of his long flannel jacket sleeves. "You feel like showing me your big muscles again?"

"I'll save that for later, Sheriff Hardass." Ronnie patted him on the chest. "I'd rather watch you do the dirty work and make smartass comments about your performance."

After filling the hole back in with sand and dirt, the three guys took turns carrying the ammo box two at a time with one on each end. Ronnie led the way while Claire brought up the rear.

As they neared the R.V. park's fence, Claire's anxiety level rose, making her stomach tighten.

Kate walked along beside her, quiet as well. "We figured out another one of Joe's mysteries."

"Sort of, but sort of not."

"What do you mean? The messages in the bullets led us to the silver bars."

"Yeah, but he left several questions unanswered." As was usual for the dead man, Claire thought with a frown.

"Such as?"

"Such as where the silver came from, when he took the bars, and why he thought it was a good steal." A rustling sound in the brush behind them made her glance over her shoulder, half expecting to see somebody holding a gun on them.

Nobody was there. It was probably just some little critter, but the shitty thing of it was now she had a whole new reason to keep watching over her shoulder.

Ah hell, she was going to turn into Ronnie, wasn't she? All skittish and squinty-eyed, waiting for the sound of a bullet to whizz by her head.

"But we can figure out those answers," Kate said, "especially with Grady helping us."

Claire nodded, still frowning. "Sure, but the biggest

question he won't be able to answer."

"What's that?"

"Who's going to come looking for the silver?" Claire looked up at the velvet black sky, wishing she could blend in with all of the stars twinkling up there. "And when?"

Chapter Ten

The next morning blew in with a storm riding on its tail. Rain and wind battered the General Store, making Claire's job of repairing some of the fence line along Jackrabbit Creek a freezing cold bitch-fest.

They'd survived another Thanksgiving dinner. Nobody had gotten sick or started a fight, and not a single person ended up stabbed with a fork. In Claire's book, that was a success, but she was damned happy to see the back side of the holiday.

After agreeing to tell Gramps and everyone else who'd stayed at the house during the treasure hunt that they'd come up empty on the search, Butch had secretly hauled the silver bars back to his place. According to Kate, they'd locked them up in the safe after noting all distinguishing numbering on each bar to give to the Sheriff.

Grady left to take his aunt home after promising Ronnie a rain check on something that made her blush and her eyes twinkle.

This morning, life was back to normal at the Dancing Winnebago R.V. Park with Deborah hung over, Chester and Manny bickering about who was faster at changing a flat tire, Ruby chastising Jess about her choice of shorts and a tank top on such a cold day, and Gramps growling at what he read in the morning paper.

"Hey, Slugger," Mac's voice cut through the wind. Zipping his coat up to his chin, he joined her along the broken fence line. "Your nose is red."

"I thought the desert was supposed to be hot and dry," she said, setting a cedar rail into place. "What's with this cold and wet crap?"

"It's called vacation weather."

Her nearly frozen ears must have heard that wrong. "What?"

"Come to Tucson with me for the weekend. It'll be like a mini-vacation."

She grabbed a screw, dropped it thanks to her cold fingers, and then picked it up again. "What's in Tucson that we don't have here in the big town of Jackrabbit Junction?"

He laughed, holding the board for her as she sank the screw and then a second one into the wood. When she finished, he ticked off on his fingers for her: "A king size bed, a large flat screen television, a boxed collection of all six seasons of *Mr. Ed*, and a bag of tamales from your favorite tamale shop."

"Oh, wow," she set her drill down. "You sure know how to sell Tucson."

"Did I mention the bed?"

She grinned. "You did."

"And your own personal masseuse?"

"That you did not mention." A freezing gust cut through her work jacket, chilling her so deeply her spine shivered.

"How about it, Slugger?" Mac pulled her into his arms, kissing the tip of her frozen nose. "You feel like taking a couple of days off for some talking-horse and beer-filled debauchery?"

"Maybe."

"What's it going to take to sway you to the dark side?"

She smiled up at him. "For starters, a kiss."

He acquiesced, warming her lips and several other partially frozen areas with his skilled touch. When he pulled back, he asked, "What else?"

"MoonPies."

"I have two boxes in the cupboard at home just waiting for you."

"Okay, but I'm going to need a naked man in bed next to me."

His smile widened. "Did you have a preference on the naked man? Because I think Chester is a big fan of *Mr. Ed*, too. We'd have to grab some *chili con carne* at the store on the way home, though, if we want to keep him happy."

"You're a funny man." She slipped her freezing cold hands up inside his jacket and shirt, plastering her palms on his warm stomach.

He sucked in a breath. "Do we have a deal?"

"Swap you for Chester in the bed and I can be packed and ready to roll in sixty minutes."

"Consider it done, Slugger."

He helped her put away her tools and load the spare fence lumber into the back of Ruby's old pickup to take back to the shed for dry keeping.

"You want to take your Jeep?" he asked.

"Nope. Kate promised to have it detailed this weekend. I left the keys with Ronnie."

"Why didn't you leave them with Kate?"

"Because she's crazy."

"Right."

An hour later, Claire was true to her word. She climbed in his pickup and shut the door. "All right, Don Juan, let the weekend of sin and depravity begin."

He leaned over and kissed her, long and slow. "I forgot to mention the bathtub," he whispered against her lips.

"I know all about the tub, McStudly."

"No, you don't." He narrowed his gaze. "But when I'm through, you will."

She captured his free hand in hers, lacing her fingers through his. "Is that a warning?"

"It's a promise, Slugger."

The End ... for now

(Note: No turkeys were harmed in the writing of this book, but the Jeep took a beating.)

Connect with Me Online

Facebook (Personal Page):
http://www.facebook.com/ann.charles.author

Facebook (Author Page):
http://www.facebook.com/pages/Ann-Charles/37302789804?ref=share

Twitter (as Ann W. Charles):
http://twitter.com/AnnWCharles

Ann Charles Website:
http://www.anncharles.com

About Ann Charles

Ann Charles is a USA Today Bestselling author who writes award-winning mysteries that are splashed with humor, romance, and whatever else she feels like throwing into the mix. When she is not dabbling in fiction, arm-wrestling with her children, attempting to seduce her husband, or arguing with her sassy cat, she is daydreaming of lounging poolside at a fancy resort with a blended margarita in one hand and a great book in the other.

BONUS READ from Ann's friend: Award-winning Author Jacquie Rogers!

Hot Work in Fry Pan Gulch

Book One of the
Honey Beaulieu—Man Hunter
Series

by Jacquie Rogers

Now, it didn't seem right that all the other business owners had paid up, and naturally the marshal was nowhere to be found, so collecting the taxes from Wakum would take a little different tactic. My brown calico dress and bonnet didn't fit my plans.

One thing he didn't know was my papa had learned me a thing or two, more than most women, or men for that matter, ever knew about shooting. So I went back to my room at the Tasty Chicken and changed to my practice clothes—buckskin britches, flannel shirt, a vest with pockets for cartridges, and my gunbelt.

Papa had given me his old Peacemakers but they were still in fine condition, oiled up plumb nice, and worked slick as a daisy. I slipped them into their holsters at my hip, tied down, and set off for Wakum's place. We was gonna have us a set-to and it would end with me collecting the tax money he owed. That's the way it was gonna be.

Twenty minutes later, I walked back into Wakum's tent and stood at the ready. He never paid a bit of mind to me and continued polishing a pistol. All right, then—I'd wait.

After a spell he said, "State your business." He still hadn't looked up yet, and I couldn't see his face for the brim of his beat-up old Stetson.

"I come to collect the taxes."

"Ain't paying."

"Then I'm taking you in."

Finally he looked at me, a flash of surprise giving him away. Papa always told me every man had a tell. Some hid theirs better than others, but they all had one, and your life could depend on whether you could read it right.

"I came here for three dollars and fifty cents."

"Little miss, I told you I'm not paying."

Well now that pissed me off—not just the "not paying" part, but especially the "little miss" part. I'm scrawny, but I'm tall as the average man. Tall as Wakum, maybe taller. I take after Papa in that regard.

"Then come with me, Mr. Wakum. You're going to jail."

"I'm staying right here. Now go on with you."

"When I leave here, either you'll be headed to jail, or I'll have your three dollars and fifty cents. Your choice."

"You're barking up the wrong tree, little miss." He pointed the pistol he'd been working so hard on and cocked it.

I didn't waste no more breath. In a flash, my gun hand pulled and fired. His beat-up hat now had a nice round hole in it.

"Shit criminy, girl!" Then he smirked. "You missed."

"I didn't miss." I held my Colt on him. "Dead men can't pay taxes, and you needed a new hat anyway."

Copyright 2016 Jacquie Rogers—All Rights Reserved

For more info on Jacquie Roger's HOT WORK IN FRY PAN GULCH and her other fun books, check out her website: www.jacquierogers.com

www.ingramcontent.com/pod-product-compliance
Lightning Source LLC
Chambersburg PA
CBHW021156080526
44588CB00008B/374